RS

PUB WA
── IN ──
Derbysh

THIRTY CIRCULAR WALKS
AROUND DERBYSHIRE INNS

Charles Wildgoose

COUNTRYSIDE BOOKS
NEWBURY, BERKSHIRE

COUNTRYSIDE BOOKS
3 Catherine Road
Newbury, Berkshire

ISBN 1 85306 277 4

For Bow

Designed by Mon Mohan
Cover illustration by Colin Doggett
Photographs and maps by the author

Produced through MRM Associates Ltd., Reading
Typeset by Paragon Typesetters, Queensferry, Clwyd
Printed in England

Contents

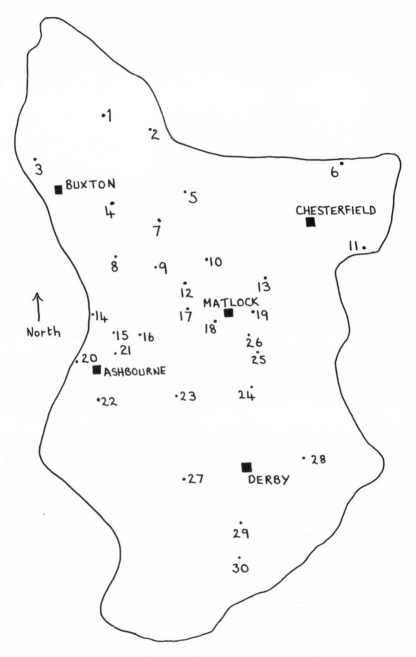

Area map showing locations of the walks.

Publisher's Note

We hope that you obtain considerable enjoyment from this book; great care has been taken in its preparation. However, changes of landlord and actual closures are sadly not uncommon. Likewise, although at the time of publication all routes followed public rights of way or well-established permitted paths, diversion orders can be made and permissions withdrawn.

We cannot accept responsibility for any inaccuracies, but we are anxious that all details covering both pubs and walks are kept up to date, and would therefore welcome information from readers which would be relevant to future editions.

Introduction

Researching this book has been the most enjoyable of experiences. Not only has it taken me to areas of Derbyshire in which I had previously walked only lightly, but it has led me to discover anew the delights of the pub lunch stop – and life will never be the same again.

The 30 walks and pubs included will, I hope, prove enjoyable to everyone buying this book. Of course, I cannot please all the people all the time but I hope I please all of you some of the time and even some of you all of the time. There are long walks and short walks, flat walks and hilly walks; there are pubs offering a comprehensive range of food and others which prefer to keep it simple.

At the time of writing each pub has signified its willingness to let you park in its own car park, provided you come in for a meal afterwards. As a matter of courtesy (and at the request of most of the landlords) ask the landlord's or landlady's permission before you use their car park – preferably the night before. They can let you know whether it will be convenient or not. I prefer to park away from the pub car park if an alternative is available as you are not then beholden to the landlord to return and have a meal if you change your mind on the walk.

Another point to bear in mind when you visit the pub is your appearance. After going for a walk I am usually hot, bothered and muddy. Please ensure that you clean yourself up – and get out of those muddy boots – before you go into the pub.

The recession is affecting many pubs. In some villages you cannot get a drink of beer some lunchtimes during the week. So do check with the pubs in good time to see if they are open on the day you want to walk. Because of the changing situation I have not listed the drinking times in the pubs. Even the mealtimes referred to in the book may change – so do check.

The walks have all been checked carefully, although some features referred to in the route description may change. The sketch map with each walk is there to give you a general impression of the route of the walk with reference to the pub. It is recommended that you take the 1:25 000 scale OS Map referred to in the text with you. You may think £3 or £4 a lot to pay for one map but each map contains many other paths that can be explored and this may be the start of an enthralling new interest for you.

Remember not to leave yourself short of time when planning your day. As a rough guide I would say allow yourself an hour for each two miles you walk. You might walk quicker than two miles an hour but part of the pleasure of walking is to be able to stand and stare. (I always say the best thing about walking is the coffee stop.) So if, for instance, you are doing the Hathersage walk (7½ or 8½ miles depending on whether the river is high or not) you would be as well to allow at least 4 or 4½ hours to complete it.

I must not finish without a mention of those who helped by checking my routes. So grateful thanks go to Jackie Gurnhill, Roy Morledge, Paul Hopkins, Paul Stanley, Frank Ogden, John Bradley, Bryan and Muriel Crapper, Greg and Elsie Boam, Judith Clay and Cynthia Normington.

Finally, a special thank you to Balkees – not just for being there on most of the walks but for just being there. Enjoy your walking.

Charles Wildgoose
spring 1994

① Hope
The Cheshire Cheese Inn

The Cheshire Cheese is a small, attractive inn, built in the 16th century. In summer flower-filled hanging baskets outside make it even more picturesque. Inside, small rooms with walls covered in horse brasses add to the charm of the place. The inn is on the old road from Cheshire, along which the cheese was brought to Derbyshire – hence the name. Years ago Cheshire cheese was actually hung in the inn. The cottage opposite was where a toll was paid for the salt which passed through on the way to being used in the making of the cheese.

The inn is popular with walkers and on a cold winter's day the hot food served at the Cheshire Cheese is very welcome. Vegetarian meals are available and you would do well to keep an eye on the 'specials' board. Yorkshire pudding with a steak and kidney filling and fidget pie are two of the more unusual meals that are served. The latter has a pastry base with layers of pork, onion and potatoes topped with hot cheese. Brewers' pie is popular as well – beef steak cooked in beer and Guinness. More traditional food, such as roast chicken, scampi and plaice, is also prepared so all tastes are catered for. Food is served from noon until 2 pm all week and from 7 pm until 9 pm Monday to Friday, 6.30 pm to 9.30 pm Saturday and 7 pm to 8.30 pm Sunday.

Wards and Stones Best Bitter are on offer, as well as draught cider. There is a beer garden, a family room and a garden area for children. Telephone: 0433 620381.

How to get there: Hope is on the A625 between Chapel-en-le-Frith and Hathersage. Once you get into the village, take the Edale road, opposite the church. The Cheshire Cheese is about 500 yards along this road, on the left.

Parking: The pub has a very small car park. Ask permission from the landlord before parking there while you walk, or, ideally, park on the street between the village and the inn. There is also a car park in the village.

Length of the walk: 4¾ miles. Map: OS Outdoor Leisure 1 The Peak District/Dark Peak Area (GR 172839).

This relatively strenuous walk takes you up into the hills above Hope. They are well worth exploring and the view from the top of Win Hill, in particular, is a good 'un. Choose a fine day and check the forecast carefully before you go – you are high up here.

The Walk
With your back to the Cheshire Cheese, turn right along the road, towards the village of Hope. The road is narrow, so take care. At the right-hand bend, pass through the squeezer stile on the left. Cross the bridge over the stream. Climb up the tarmac lane, passing the Peak and Northern Footpath Society signpost No 122. Pass under the railway and then bear left towards Fullwood Stile Farm. On the way up the tarmac drive, pass the end of the driveway leading to The Pastures. Then, approximately 30 yards later, take the left fork, ignoring the drive to The Homestead. By now the lane has more of a 'packed' surface rather than a tarmac one. Keep to the right of the Coach House. Walk through the stone squeezer stile, keeping along the wall side through the first field. Ahead to the left is Lose Hill. Keep straight on through the second field with the fence on your right. At the farm buildings, pass through the stile to the left of the gate. Turn left, then right, then left through the farm, to come out on a lane beyond. Ascend this lane, passing the Fullwood Stile Farm sign.
Stay on the track until you come to a gate on to open moorland. Pass through the gate, keeping to the main track – ignore the path to the right. You slowly ascend until you are on a similar level to Lose Hill on the opposite side of the valley. Immediately to the right of Lose Hill is the Kinder Scout plateau. Just under a mile from Fullwood Stile

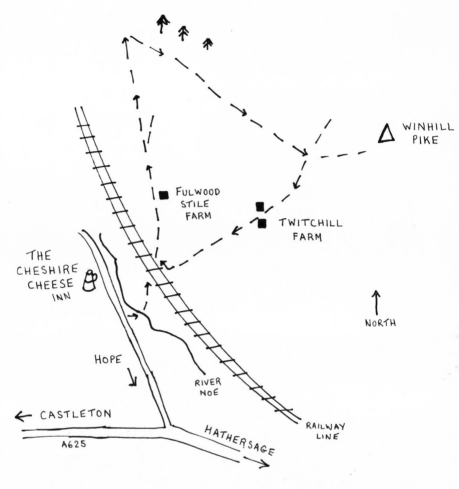

Farm you come to another gate. Do not pass through, but turn back
to the right at an acute angle and walk towards the trees on the hillside
ahead. Ignore the track to the left which runs parallel to the wall you
are walking away from. The track you are now on is a bridleway with
a smooth, grassy surface.

As you slowly ascend on the bridleway there are trees to your left.
To your right can be seen the large, ugly chimney of the cement works
in the valley. The bridleway reaches a wall and you walk alongside it
for quite a way. Stay on the grassy track, leaving the trees and heading
towards a wall with a gap in it. Follow the track as it continues uphill.
In front of you is the easily recognisable shape of Winhill Pike, the

highest part of Win Hill itself. Down to your left Ladybower Reservoir and Ashopton Viaduct should be visible on a clear day.

The track you are on levels out and comes to the edge of a wall. Keep this on your right and Win Hill in front of you, slightly to the left. At the end of the wall, head forward. You come to a crossroads of paths, with a signpost pointing along all four tracks. You need to take the path downhill to the right, signposted to Lose Hill, Hope and Aston. However, if you want to admire the view from Winhill Pike, carry straight forward to the trig point. The views are well worth it, although it can be very exposed right at the top.

After returning to the crossroads of paths, take the one downhill towards Lose Hill, Hope and Aston. This path at first heads roughly in the direction of the cement works chimney below. Walk past the stone cairns as you proceed diagonally down the hillside. Climb over the step-over stile and press on in the direction of the farm driveway further down the hillside. Keep straight ahead towards a metal gate and fingerpost, passing to the right of the wood below. After going through the metal gate, you will come down to Twitchill Farm. Walk between the buildings and down the farm drive. At the bottom of the drive, turn right and walk parallel to the railway line on your left. Go left under the railway and back to the lane, retracing your steps to the Cheshire Cheese.

Hathersage
The Scotsman's Pack

Hathersage is one of the busier villages in the Peak District. The Scotsman's Pack inn is next to the village school just down the road from the church of St Michael and All Angels, where Little John (Robin Hood's right-hand man) is buried. Little John's chair is actually owned by the pub – you can see it as you enter. The village also has connections with Charlotte Brontë, as she stayed at Hathersage Vicarage in 1845. A couple of years later she wrote *Jane Eyre* and there seems little doubt that she used the surname of a local Derbyshire family, the Eyres, who lived nearby.

The Scotsman's Pack stands on one of the old roads leading from Derbyshire into Sheffield. It was a regular stopping place for travellers, including packmen frae Scotland who sold their tweeds locally. There is little left of the original building, and the present inn dates from the 1930s. It is fairly spacious inside with a good-sized bar and plenty of seating. The food is served from noon to 2 pm every day and 6 pm to 9 pm Monday to Saturday (7 pm to 9 pm on Sunday). The landlady makes the home-made dishes and all the vegetables are fresh. There are vegetarian dishes, mixed grill, steak, chicken and ham pie, lasagne, moussaka and curries. Real ale fans are catered for with Burtonwood

Bitter, James Forshaw's and Burtonwood Dark Mild. Strongbow Dry Cider is on offer too. The inn has a no-smoking area, a beer garden, a family room, a garden area for children, and some accommodation. Telephone: 0433 650253/650712.

How to get there: Hathersage is on the A625, just 8 miles south-west of Sheffield. The Scotsman's Pack lies on School Lane, which runs from the top of the main village street towards the church.

Parking: The car park is quite small, so it is best to park either on the road nearby or in the village at the main car park (well signed).

Length of the walk: 7½ miles, if you can cross the river by the stepping stones. If not, say 8½ miles. Maps: OS Outdoor Leisure 24 The Peak District/White Peak Area, and Pathfinder 743 Sheffield (GR 34817).

The walk up the valley to Abney is delightful, the view of the Hope valley as you come to Offerton Edge is breathtaking and the stepping stones are fun! Do not try and cross them, though, if the water level is high.

Nottinghamshire lays claim to Robin Hood but Sherwood Forest extended into Derbyshire, so perhaps Robin and his Merrie Men used to frequent these parts. As you travel round Derbyshire you will find no end of references to Robin Hood.

The Walk
From the pub, turn to the left towards the village. At the intersection, turn right and walk down the main street, passing Longlands and the George Hotel. Keep straight ahead to pass Brookfield Manor and walk along the Castleton road towards the railway bridge. Pass under this and turn left at an acute angle, walking to the left of the tumbledown barn. Cross the field towards the right-hand side of the buildings opposite. Go through the stile and over the stream to the road. Turn right and walk round the corner. Just beyond the house standing on its own, dated 1873, and past the entrance to Nether Hall, turn right down the track off the tarmac drive. Follow the track down the right-hand side of the first field, crossing the stile at the end. Stay on the right-hand side of the second field to follow this well-used path to the road at Leadmill Bridge.

Turn right over the bridge and, just as you come to the Plough, turn right up the lane, signposted 'Abney 2½'. This climbs gradually, giving good views of Hathersage on the right. At the field corner, about 200 yards beyond the farmhouse, take the track to the left. Walk down this and bear left on the path, crossing a cattle grid. This path takes you down a steepish bank through hawthorn trees and continues across an unspoilt meadow to a stone bridge.

13

After crossing the bridge, walk up the field to the top left corner. Pass through the squeezer stile at the old gate and walk straight on up the track. On your left is Hazelford Hall. When you reach the top of this track, turn right along another. Pass on the top side of a farm (Tor Farm) as you head up the valley. Go through the gate just in front of the barn and continue along the track, heading towards the conifers ahead. This track leads to a gate into a field. After passing through, keep on the track through three fields, then enter a newly planted area of trees. Continue through the trees, taking the left-hand path at the fork – ignore the path dropping down to the right. When you reach a junction of two streams in a lovely wooded valley, climb the stile and cross the stream to the signpost. This was erected by the Peak and Northern Footpath Society in 1989, and tells you that the path you are on goes via Stoke Ford to Abney. Take the track leading up to the left from the signpost and climb out of the valley bottom. Where it bears sharply left, keep straight ahead along the less well defined track. At this point, it is worth looking behind you. Higger Tor and the various Edges are clearly visible in the distance. At the gateposts further along, drop down into the small valley and out the other side. Stay on the path until it descends to Stoke Ford. There is another Peak and Northern signpost here, this one erected in 1939. After crossing the bridge, turn right and go over another. Turn left up the track, signposted 'Abney' – ignore the signpost to the Leadmill-Abney road to the right.

You are now on a well-defined track between conifers and silver birch trees. Keep on this for the next ½ mile or so. Eventually it climbs away from the valley bottom and brings you into Abney. At the road, turn right and walk away from the village beyond Lane End Farm. Climb the ladder stile on the left where the road bends slightly right, then keep ahead to the stile at the side of the gateway, 30 yards away. Stay on the right-hand side of the field. Bear right over the next stile and continue to the one beyond. The valley to your right is the one you have just walked up.

Stay on the green track through the heather of Offerton Moor. Keep straight on when the path is crossed by another and continue for some distance until you come out on Offerton Edge, above Hathersage to the right. What a view! On your left is Win Hill, Ladybower Reservoir and the plateau of Kinder Scout. The path bears diagonally right, down the hillside towards Offerton Hall some way down the hill. You should come out just to the right of the hall, on a track. Turn left and walk down past the hall. This was one of seven apparently owned by the Eyre family. Walk over the cobbled area and then onto a tarmac drive. Just before you drop down the lane, turn right through the gate at the side of a line of well-established beech trees. Keep down the left

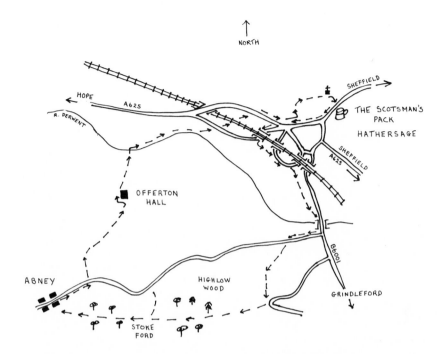

side of the field to cross the stile, then go straight ahead to the gateway below. Walk down to the river, behind the three-fingered signpost, and cross the stepping stones. If they are flooded walk down-river to Leadmill Bridge and retrace the outward route, back into Hathersage.

Once you are over the stepping stones, turn right along the river bank for 500 yards. Where it bears right, you should bear left to a gate at the side of the busy road ahead. Cross to the stile opposite, then go half-right to the railway line. Take care as this is still used. Once over the railway, walk half-right to a quieter road. Turn right along this, passing an old millstone, and descend to the main road. Walk up the left side, then turn left at the post office into Besom Lane. Pass the National Westminster bank on your right and continue to a track. Turn left along this. After just over 100 yards, you reach some playing fields on your left. Turn right, towards the church, along the Shuttleworth Memorial Walk. This leads into the churchyard. On your right as you reach the porch is the grave of Little John, between the 10 ft high yew trees. The church is well worth exploring and usually open. Leave the churchyard by the lychgate, turn right down the lane and follow it as it bears right, back to the Scotsman's Pack.

③ Fernilee
The Shady Oak

The Shady Oak is a rather striking building on the A5004. Inside there are photographs of the pub before it became a pub. There is a taproom for fans of darts and dominoes and also a larger room where you can replenish yourself after the walk. The staff are friendly and the pub seems to be popular with locals as well as visitors – whether walkers or not. Probably the only Boddingtons pub in the book, the Shady Oak sells Boddingtons Bitter and Mild plus Draught Strongbow Cider.

The menu states that 'hikers and motorists alike will find a cosy resting place, a convivial atmosphere and an appetising, wholesome table at the Shady Oak'. How nice to feel so welcome after a good walk. The landlord is keen to encourage walkers and has even prepared a leaflet of 'Shady Walks' – others to enjoy next time you are in the area. Besides welcoming walkers, the menu deals with food, of course. Grills, home-made pies and quiches, roasts, fish, quick snacks, a children's menu, cold dishes, sandwiches and sweets are all covered. The sort of meals you can expect are fillet steak, savoury minced beef pie, roast beef, grilled whole trout, steak and onion muffin, fish fingers, chips and beans (from the children's menu) and home-cooked tongue salad. There is plenty more to choose from, including daily specials on the blackboard. Lunch is served from 11.30 am to 2.15 pm (from noon on a Sunday). Evening meals are from 7 pm to 9.30 pm (Sunday to Tuesday) and 6 pm to 9.30 pm (Wednesday to Saturday).

Telephone: 0663 732212.

How to get there: The Shady Oak is on the A5004, which runs north-west from Buxton to Whaley Bridge. Travelling from Buxton, the pub is on the right, about 2 miles before Whaley Bridge.

Parking: Parking is available at the pub, and there is also a layby 300 yards down the road from the Shady Oak on the Whaley Bridge side of the pub.

Length of the walk: 6 miles. Map: OS Outdoor Leisure 24 The Peak District/White Peak Area (GR 016790).

This is an attractive walk through the Goyt valley. A chance to wander through broadleaf woodland, conifers and by the side of Fernilee Reservoir. You will encounter nothing too strenuous and the route is through changing scenery.

The Walk

Cross the road in front of the pub. Head down the track opposite, following the footpath sign. When you come to a farm, walk through it to the gate at the far end. Cross the stile. Bear half-left towards a stile, 20 yards left of a small gate across the field. In the next field the path descends straight towards a small wooden footbridge. From here walk to a larger footbridge across the field in front of you. After you have crossed this second bridge, turn right. Walk through the Derbyshire Wildlife Trust nature reserve; Hillbridge Wood. Follow the path through the woodland for 500 yards, eventually moving away from the river Goyt.

Come out of the reserve into a field and walk towards two gateposts. As you reach them, turn left at an acute angle along the track towards the line of trees running towards Overton Hall Farm. As you reach the trees cross a stile, then a tiny stream. Follow the path on the far side as it bears right, then left, near three oak trees. At the end of the field go through the gateway, and bear right, uphill, alongside a wall. The view to your left opens out and the Shady Oak is visible across the valley. The track brings you to another gate. Cross the stile there and walk to the track in front. Take the fork to the left and walk past Madscar Farm. Once through the gate beyond the farm, follow the track to the valley bottom. From here, turn left up the track

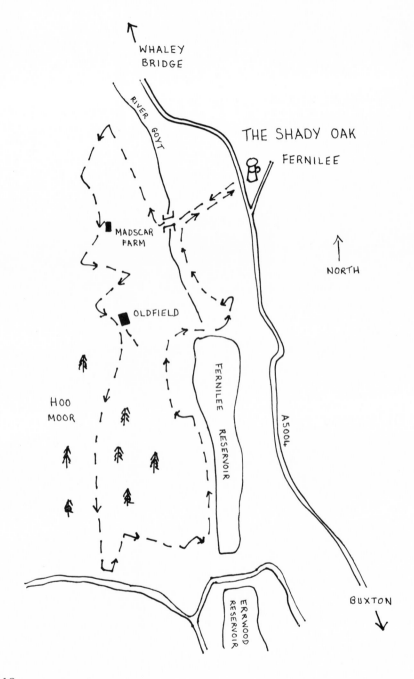

WHALEY
BRIDGE

RIVER GOYT

THE SHADY OAK

FERNILEE

MADSCAR
FARM

OLDFIELD

NORTH

HOO
MOOR

FERNILEE RESERVOIR

A5004

BUXTON

ERRWOOD RESERVOIR

18

towards Knipe Farm. About 75 yards before the farm, take the gate on your right that leads into a field. Walk along the track through the field and pass a small walled conifer plantation on your left, towards a gate. Go through this and turn left along the walled track.

Pass the collection of farm buildings on your left – Normanwood. Take the gateway on the left at the end of the field. Follow the track, with silver birches and fir trees on your left. You should now be able to see Fernilee Reservoir to your left. Pass through the gate into the property known as Oldfield, then go through the gate at the far side of the farm. Here the track forks, left down to the reservoir or right to Hoo Moor. Head right for the moor. The track soon leads you into Forestry Commission property as you walk between silver birches and conifers. Follow this for a mile until you reach a road. Just before the road, at the gate, turn left through the gap.

Follow the descending path between the wall and the fence at the waymark. Turn right at the end of the fence to walk straight ahead for 350 yards, descending as you go. At the T-junction of paths, turn left into the woodland. Follow this path as it bears right, downhill, through the conifers. This brings you to Fernilee Reservoir. Turn left along the side of the water.

The path is quite easy to follow. About 700 yards later, after crossing a stream, the path splits into three. Take the one uphill to the left (at the yellow waymark with a '3'). Climb alongside the stream, bear right and follow the path to a seat. This was placed here by Martin Watson of Buxton in October 1975 'for the benefit of country lovers'.

Turn right along the path and follow it for ½ mile through the wood. At the end, turn right on the tarmac track towards the reservoir. Cross the road over the reservoir bank. Turn left at the far side, along the straight tarmac road. Then turn sharp left, ignoring the 'No unauthorised vehicle' sign. This road bears left, then right.

.Eventually, you come to the North West Water Works. Keep on the track through the works, then straight ahead on the gravel track into the trees beyond. Pass over the stile at the side of a gate. The track fizzles out, but keep on alongside the river, crossing another stile (with a dog gate at the side). This brings you back to the larger of the two footbridges you crossed at the start of the walk.

Bear right to the first footbridge you crossed, then retrace your steps back to the Shady Oak.

Taddington
The Queen's Arms

With a cellar that has been used as a mortuary, the Queen's Arms has a history – and people are still dying to try the good food on sale there. Live walkers are welcome and with fresh home-cooked meals (including Tennessee Grasshopper Pie – a peppermint mousse which should put a spring in your step) it is not to be missed. The pub aims to give value for money and relies on traditional food to do this. The scampi, gammon, steak, sandwiches and roast beef are all excellent, as are the specials such as coq-au-vin. Meals are served from noon until 2 pm and from 7 pm to 9 pm every day, although the menu is reduced on a Sunday evening. In addition to the Tetley Bitter a guest beer is also available. The draught cider is Merrydown. The Queen's Arms like many pubs is quieter during the winter months. With the lure of open log fires it is well worth visiting then. The pub comprises two rooms – one a taproom (with pool, darts and dominoes) and the other a lounge/dining area. There is also a beer garden and a family room.
  Telephone: 0298 85245.

How to get there: Taddington is 6 miles east of Buxton. The village is well signposted from the A6. Stay on the village street to reach the pub.

Parking: With permission, you can park in the pub car park while you walk. There is also parking on the village street nearby.

Length of the walk: 6 miles. Map: OS Outdoor Leisure 24 The Peak District/White Peak Area (GR 145710).

Three villages are linked by this walk – Taddington, Flagg and Chelmorton. All are basically one-street communities, typical of so many in this part of the Peak District. The ancient field system around Chelmorton is interesting and so are the old water lanes in Taddington. There is also a glorious view back over Taddington after you have climbed out of it. Choose a clear day, if you can.

The Walk

From the Queen's Arms, walk straight ahead up the track opposite, at the side of a garage, and continue uphill. The track becomes a narrow walled path. Bear round to the left at the top. Almost immediately climb up the bank to the right. Pass through the stile into the small field complete with swings and playground. Walk along the bottom of the hill above the walled path, which is to your right, then zig-zag up to the shelter. Sit down and enjoy the view in front of you – you will probably welcome a breather at this point. Follow the path past the top side of the playground, then walk to the left of the walled well. Follow the path uphill to the stile, which brings you out on to the road.

Turn left on the road – again there are good views back over Taddington. About 450 yards later, just past the road turn-off to the right, take the stile on the right and walk diagonally across the field to the far corner and the gateway. Once through this gateway, walk round the bottom of the mound in the field to the steps over the wall. In the next field keep straight ahead through the middle. Cross through the narrow field and go diagonally to the far right-hand corner of the next field and the gateway there. Then head for, and pass through, the next gateway, 40 or 50 yards further on. Walk past the mound on your left to the stile at the gateway. Bear just slightly left to the stile in the field beyond, then left down the narrow field to the road.

At the road, turn right and, 75 yards later, turn left at the signpost. Walk straight through the field towards Flagg, passing under the electricity lines. The stretch of path through this field is approximately 550 yards long. As you come to the end, aim 25 yards or so to the right

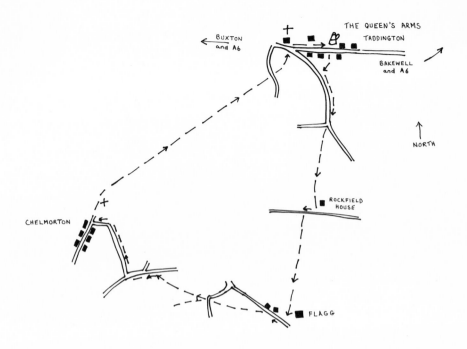

THE QUEEN'S ARMS
TADDINGTON

BUXTON
and A6

BAKEWELL
and A6

NORTH

ROCKFIELD
HOUSE

CHELMORTON

FLAGG

of the line of trees heading away from you. Go through the stile into the newly planted croft near the pond. Climb the two wooden stiles to the right of the pond, then walk towards the left-hand side of the field, towards Flagg Hall in front of you. Go through the gateway and the farmyard beyond, then down the drive towards the road.

Turn right along the road, past the school, and continue through Flagg, passing the post office and stores on the right. Look out for steps over the wall on your left (to the right of a gate and just before the chapel). Climb over the stile and head right, towards the copse of trees. The path is quite well defined at this point and the steps of the next stile are visible. Climb these and head straight on towards the copse. To its left, in the corner, there is a stile to climb over. Be careful, as this can be slippery when wet. Walk alongside the wood on your right for just a few yards. Climb over the next stile and follow the path. Keeping another smallish copse on your left, walk to the end of the field and climb the stile over the wall to the left of the gateway. Go over the next stile and head directly towards the farm in front. At the signpost, negotiate the stile. Cross the road and climb into the next field.

Walk up the field and cross the step-over stile at the side of the gate in front. In the next field, keep to the right of the humps, then pass through the gateway to the left of a small wood. In the next field, walk half-right to the stile in the wall, then walk to the far corner of the subsequent field. In the field beyond this, bear right and proceed to the tree in the right-hand wall – the stile is to the left of the tree. Walk half-left uphill, following the path, which is reasonably clear on the ground. Head for the corner of the wall projecting into the field in front of you. Once you reach this, keep on towards the far corner of the field and the road. Turn left. Ignore the first right turn, but take the second lane (beyond the 'Chelmorton' sign). Follow this road for 700 yards. It is reasonably quiet, with good views to the left, including the narrow fields of the medieval field system. At the T-junction, turn right uphill, past the house with '1869' on it, and carry on to the Church Inn.

From the inn walk uphill on the tarmac road, which soon ends and becomes a rough track. Take the right fork and stay with it as it ascends. Behind can be seen the village of Chelmorton and the unusual weather vane on the church spire. The track becomes a field path and passes through a long, narrow field full of bumps and hollows. These are the remains of leadmining, which has been carried on for hundreds (if not thousands) of years in the White Peak area of Derbyshire. In springtime look out for the wild pansies near this path.

Stay on the path through the narrow field for over 400 yards, before leaving it at the far right corner. After negotiating the stile, turn right and then, almost immediately, left. Follow the line of the signpost for Taddington and cross the field ahead, to the stile which is to the right of the farm (Five Wells Farm). Once over the stile, walk through the next three fields alongside the wall on your left. Cross over the track and keep straight on along the wallside for the next six fields. After passing a trig point (over the wall to your left), you come to a raised underground reservoir. Cross the stile to the right of this and then walk diagonally across the field to the right, towards the signpost. A view of Taddington village opens out below you. Climb over the stile and walk towards the church spire. Keep straight ahead and drop downhill towards the road.

Cross the road to the stile opposite and then, a few yards later, go through the next stile. The path now goes straight on, bearing left behind the tree near the houses. Walk down the footpath between the conifer hedge and the wall. At the road, walk downhill towards the church. After a few yards, turn right and walk through the village. All the houses are different – as in many villages hereabouts there is no sign of uniformity. You then come back to the Queen's Arms, on the left.

Calver
5
The Bridge Inn

The Bridge Inn at Calver is 150 years old and part of it was originally an alehouse for the local leadminers. It is very well positioned for walks in all directions. Less than a mile to the east are the Edges – Froggatt Edge, Curbar Edge and Baslow Edge – which form an irregular line of gritstone rock, rising to the moorland above the Derwent valley. Further north are Bamford and Stanage Edges, all of them popular with climbers of all standards. From the Bridge Inn you can walk south towards Baslow and the gentler countryside around Chatsworth, or westwards along the more barren area of Longstone Edge. Northwards are wooded valleys full of delightful scenery. The Bridge is, therefore, a pub to be visited again and again.

The food at this busy but roomy pub certainly merits regular visits. Besides dishes like home-made quiche, Cumberland sausage and broccoli and cheese pie, look out for the specials on the blackboard. These change daily but usually feature vegetarian dishes such as tuna and pasta bake, leek and mushroom crumble, and spinach and mushroom lasagne. Lunch is from noon to 2 pm, with the evening meal from 6.30 pm to 8.30 pm (Tuesday to Saturday inclusive) and on Sunday from 7 pm to 8 pm. No food is served on Monday evening.

The real ales are Hardys & Hansons Kimberley Classic and Best Bitter. Dry Blackthorn and Autumn Gold are the draught ciders. There is a beer garden (very popular in summer) as well as a no-smoking section and a garden area for children.
Telephone: 0433 630415.

How to get there: The Bridge stands just off the A623, which runs from Baslow, 10 miles west of Chesterfield, to Chapel-en-le-Frith, north of Buxton. The inn is about 1½ miles from Baslow, on the right-hand side near the school.

Parking: There is a cul-de-sac in front of Curbar school and street parking nearby. If you want to use the pub car park while you walk, ask the landlord first.

Length of the walk: 6 miles. Map: OS Outdoor Leisure 24 The Peak District/White Peak Area (GR 247744).

A route with a bit of everything – history, interesting buildings, woodland, fields, a couple of villages and some gentle uphill walking, opening up magnificent views.

The Walk
Walk along Dukes Drive, the road opposite the pub entrance. On the left is Calver Mill, which was used to represent the prison in the TV series *Colditz*. The river Derwent is just over the wall. Take the footpath on the left at the end of a wall, at the signpost marked 'New Bridge'. Follow the path alongside the river. Just before you reach the road bridge, there is a lovely view downstream across the river, towards Curbar Edge on the horizon. Cross the road to the stile opposite and continue upstream, with the river on your left, for just under ½ mile. Climb over the stile on to the road and turn left. This brings you to Froggatt Bridge.
    Cross this and continue up the road for 400 yards to the old toll bar cottage. Cross the road, pass through the stile and walk straight up the field. It is worthwhile to turn round at this point to admire the wide view behind you. Along the horizon are the Edges where many well known climbers have gained experience. Climb the stile next to the gate. Proceed up the right-hand side of the field to the road. Walk for a few yards along the road to the left, then cross to the gate and pass through the stile. Walk up the right-hand side of the field, along the track, towards the trees on the hilltop. This is not shown on maps as a footpath, being, in fact, a road! On the White Peak map it is shown as a black dotted track, which joins the western end of a footpath. There is nothing to indicate it passing through the wood to the track

25

running from Top Riley (a farm) down to Eyam village. On the ground, however, it is definitely there. Pass through the gate at the top of the field and follow the walled track into the wood. This leads to a path cutting in from the right. Turn left along this path, climbing slowly as you go. The path soon levels out and you are walking between beech trees, with an attractive view to the left.

At the end of the wood, turn left down the track. About 200 yards further on is a tiny National Trust property in the field to your right. These are the Riley Graves. The family buried there are all Hancocks – Riley refers to the name of the area.

Continue along the track, downhill, to the outskirts of Eyam (pronounced 'Eem'). Where the track joins the road, continue to the right into the village. The road bears first left, then right. On the right-hand bend look for the notice on the building, roughly 10 ft off the ground. This tells you something about Miner's Arms Croft. In the same block of buildings but just round the corner, look out for the old window in the cottage known as Sunnyside. On the side of the Eyam Tea Rooms another sign tells you this used to be the Bold Rodney Inn.

Turn left at the telephone box, into Lydgate. Another sign tells you how the men in the village used to stand 'watch and ward' from 9 pm to 6 am – an early form of Neighbourhood Watch perhaps. Proceed up Lydgate, passing more graves on your right. Where it opens out, keep straight on towards the gate in front. Pass through the stile at the side of the gate and walk down the track. Stay on this through two fields. At the end of the second one, take the stile at the side of the track and walk along the walled path. Beyond this, keep straight on through the field. The path is clear and you pass the boundary stone on your left. This is where the villagers of Stoney Middleton used to leave food every day for the plague-stricken Eyam villagers in 1665 – 6, when three-quarters of the 350 or so villagers died.

From the stone, the path drops downhill to give you a splendid view of Stoney Middleton below. The path comes to the far corner of the field. Then turn right along the tarmac track between the cottages. Pass the telephone box on the right. At the bottom of the hill (known as The Bank), turn left towards the church, 100 yards away. Turn left in front of the church, passing Church View on the left and Spa Cottage on the right.

Bear right and continue along the track, passing the Roman Baths. In spite of the name, there is no evidence that the Romans actually built them. The spring that supplies the water has a constant temperature of 63° Fahrenheit. At the end of the high wall on your right, where the track bears left, pass through the kissing-gate. Walk on through the field for 200 yards, into the open field. On the left are electricity poles. Head uphill, slightly to the left, towards the end of

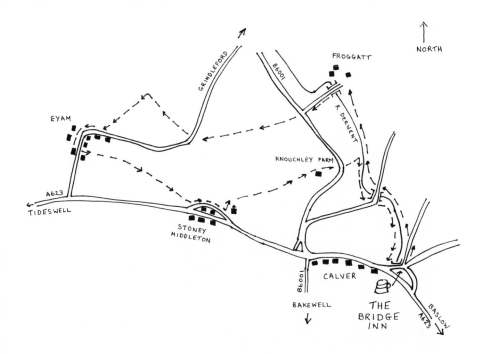

the field. This takes you into some hawthorn trees and then alongside a wall on your left. To your right is Calver Sough and Hare Knoll. Cross the wall and walk towards Knouchley Farm ahead, keeping to the left-hand side of the buildings. The path passes to the left of a cowshed, to join a track from the left. Turn right on the track, going through the stile at the side of the gate behind the old barn, and stay on it, passing a newish farmhouse on the right. Walk down the drive to the road.

Cross the stile opposite and walk down the left side of the field towards the river. At the bottom of the field, pass through the gateway on the left and walk down to the water, where you turn right. Follow the river downstream for 450 yards, crossing a footbridge and stream as you do so. Climb up to the road at the bridge, but watch out for cars from both sides. Cross to the signpost marked 'Calver Bridge' and walk down the track. Where the track fizzles out after 500 yards or so in the field, continue towards the buildings in front. These are surmounted by a bell tower. At the side of these buildings, take the kissing-gate at the gates (erected in memory of the Reverend Leslie Jacques of Wakefield). Follow the track until it comes to the road. Turn left here, over the old bridge, to the Bridge Inn.

Eckington
The Mossbrook

The Mossbrook can be no more than 5 or 6 miles from the centre of Sheffield, and Eckington itself is surrounded by industry and coalmines, and yet this pub walk is fascinating. It is an oasis in this fairly industrial area and shows you do not have to travel far out of town into the Peak District to have an enjoyable and scenic walk.

The oldest part of the pub – now an attractive bar area – used to be a house, and the landlord has a photograph of the building as it once was. The recent extension has been very well done giving the appearance inside of an old building with exposed beams. In all this is an attractive and welcoming place.

The comprehensive menu in this Beefeater pub features such starters as pork satay or oriental ocean combo (scallops and white fish pieces in a crumb coating). For main courses there are, for example, steaks, including 6 oz or 8 oz sirloin steak, hoisin pork fillet and salmon and South Sea kebab. You will have detected an oriental influence, but you can still get gammon steak, minted lamb, roast Lincolnshire duck or steak and kidney pie, if you want something simpler. Then there are a couple of vegetarian dishes, five dishes for younger guests and also mouthwatering desserts (brandy snap

corruption and banana nirvana being only two). Finally, eleven coffees are on offer. The real ales – Castle Eden, Flowers IPA, Boddingtons and Marston's Pedigree – are good too. The draught ciders are Strongbow and Woodpecker. There is a small garden area for children and a patio.
Telephone: 0246 432771.

How to get there: The Mossbrook is on the Sheffield road (the A616) on the north-east side of Eckington, 1½ miles from Mosborough.

Parking: The pub car park is available if you want to start your walk there, but let the landlord know first. There is ample alternative parking in Eckington itself.

Length of the walk: 5¾ miles. Map: OS Pathfinder 744 Aughton and Carlton in Lindrick and a small section of 762 Worksop (South) and Staveley (GR 434799).

This is quite an easy walk, and one of interesting contrasts, with the route passing through the lovely Moss valley, the edge of Mosborough and the outskirts of Eckington.

The Walk
From the Mossbrook, turn left to the traffic lights, then turn right, following the signpost for Eckington and Whittington, along Church Street. Walk straight on between the White Hart and the church of St Peter and St Paul. Pass Church Farm on the left as the road bears right then left downhill. Pass the Millhouse on the right. The road enters a wood. Follow it as it turns right, crossing the Moss brook (the watercourse not the pub). You will find that you cross and recross this brook a number of times on the walk. Take the stile at the side of the metal gate near the car park.

This leads you on to a track that rises slowly through the woodland. Ignore the path crossing it. You then head through more open country but with trees and shrubs on either side. At the end of the field on your left, where the wood starts, the path divides. Take the left fork down to the footbridge, 60 yards away. Cross it and, after 40 yards (ignoring the tracks to the left and straight ahead), take the track to the right. This soon passes some fairly substantial beech trees. The path forks after 500 yards. Ignoring the track rising to the left, descend to the right. This leads you alongside a field on your left and into the open. About 400 yards away at the end of the field, bear right to cross the Moss by another footbridge.

Keep on the path running away from the bridge and, after 100 yards or so, keep to the left of the pond. Stay on this path as it meanders

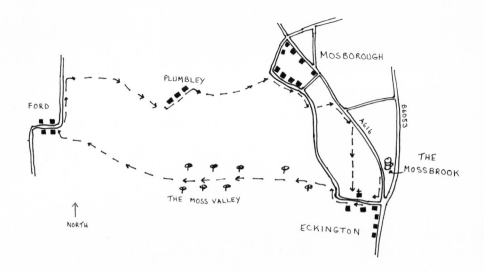

alongside the brook on your left. As the path comes near to the brook, take the stile to the right and go over the small cement slab bridge. Still walking upstream with the Moss on your left, the path leads to another pond, with a sign erected by the Ford Angling Club. At the end of the pond, walk through the car park. Head out on to the road with the Bridge Inn on your left. You will probably by now have noticed the waymarks with the mouse on. These show the route of the Mosborough Country Walk – a 10 mile walk in the area.

Turn right for 300 yards, passing Oak House on the opposite side of the road. Take the track to the right (about 75 yards beyond Oak House). Stay on this bridlepath with the Moss valley down to the right. Follow the bridleway for 500 yards from the road, until it bears left and descends to a number of signposts on the left. The bridleway then rises from these signposts. Ignoring two paths to the right, you eventually come to Plumbley, a largish farm complex. Just beyond this, turn right down the track, slowly descending as you go.

Keep on the cinder track as you pass Plumbley Lane Farm on the right. The bridleway now runs across the bottom of a number of allotment gardens and the back gardens of a row of houses. At the Wheel, keep straight on through the hawthorn and holly to come out with Westwell Garage on your right. Pass Plumbley Hall Mews on the right and bear left on the road. Turn right at the end of Plumbley Hall Road into Chapel Street. This takes you past a large grass triangle near Mosborough Methodist church. Pass the fish and chip shop on the opposite side of the street to bear slightly right into South Street.

30

Keep straight on past some interesting houses on the left. About 200 yards beyond The Alma, take the footpath along the track to the left, beside the house numbered '88', then take the waymarked path between the walls. This path eventually passes between very high walls, with Eckington Hall to the right, although you cannot see it until later.

Turn right on the road to slowly descend. As you return into Derbyshire, take the path along the level as the road goes down to your left. This will be the sixth time on this walk that you have crossed the boundary between Derbyshire and South Yorkshire. After 250 yards take the steps descending to the right and then follow this path for 450 yards to cross the Moss (again), before ascending to the church.

Beyond the church, turn left past the White Hart to the traffic lights, 250 yards later. Turn left, back to the Mossbrook.

Ashford-in-the-Water
The Ashford Hotel

The Ashford Hotel is an 18th century coaching house standing on a street corner in the picturesque village of Ashford-in-the-Water, just 1½ miles west of Bakewell (where the puddings, as they are called locally, come from). Many visitors are drawn here to see the picturesque Sheepwash Bridge, 300 yards up the road from the hotel, past the church. Originally the bridge was on an old packhorse route but it got its name because farmers washed their sheep in the river Wye at this point before they were sheared. It is one of the prettiest spots in the area and is featured in many photographs and paintings. Each year in Ashford on the Saturday before Trinity Sunday the local wells are 'dressed' or decorated, well-dressing being a tradition largely peculiar to Derbyshire. There are indications that the custom dates back to Celtic times, over 2,000 years ago, and would probably have been to give thanks for the water from the well. If you want to visit the village to view the wells, the Tourist Information Centre at Bakewell will give you details.

The Ashford Hotel has quite a spacious interior with a relaxed ambience. The food at this friendly hotel is fresh and home cooked by six chefs. The palate may be tempted with dishes such as North Sea codling, lemon sole Breton, tortelloni formaggio (pasta filled with ricotta cheese and cooked in a red wine sauce with tomatoes and basil) and chicken with leek and Stilton sauce. Food is available from noon until 9 pm daily. The village gets very busy at holiday times and weekends, so bear this in mind if you wish to have a meal here. Real ale fans can sample Stones and Bass Bitter as well as the rarer Ashford Bitter.

Telephone: 0629 812725.

How to get there: Ashford lies between Bakewell and Buxton. Head north off the A6 along the A6020, then turn left, just over 250 yards later. The hotel is on your left as you enter the village.

Parking: There are no objections to you using the hotel car park, while you walk. There is so much parking available on the streets nearby, however, that it is just as easy to park away from the hotel.

Length of the walk: 4¼ miles. Map: OS Outdoor Leisure 24 The Peak District/White Peak Area (GR 197697).

A fairly steady walk through the village and then along an ancient track leads to one of the finest and best-known panoramas in Derbyshire. From Monsal Head there is an impressive view of the Monsal Dale Viaduct down below. The return route to Ashford passes through fields and across the Monsal Trail to lead you back to the Ashford Hotel and a chance to refuel.

The Walk
Walk from the Ashford Hotel along Church Street, passing the Bull's Head and some attractive houses near to the church. Continue until you reach a shelter on your left. Just beyond this (also on the left) is the lovely old Sheepwash Bridge, where fish are usually waiting for titbits in the waters of the Wye below. Turn right along Fennel Street. At the grass triangle at the end of the street, bear right up Vicarage Lane. Within 50 yards take the footpath signposted 'Monsal Dale', to the left. Climb up the steps past the houses on the right until you come out into open fields. From the squeezer stile, walk straight ahead

33

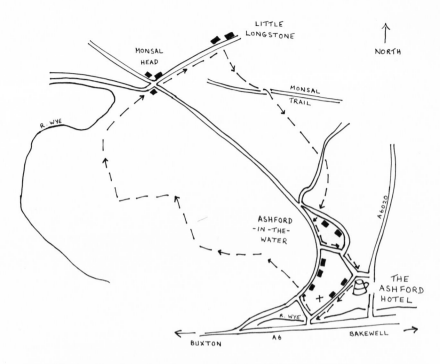

towards the far right-hand corner of the field, over 300 yards away. Keep slightly to the left of the two hawthorn trees just over halfway into the field. As you walk nearer the end of this field, the stile should be visible at the far end of the hawthorn hedge.

Once on to the rough track, Pennyunk Lane, turn left. Walk past the white-painted bungalow, Ploverfield. At the pond on your left, follow the track to the right for the next ½ mile, ignoring tracks off it to the right. The track ends at a gate. Climb over the stile beside it and walk up the left-hand side of the field. Climb over the stile at the top of the field and immediately turn right. Join another track 50 yards away and follow it for 500 yards until you come out above Monsal Dale, after climbing a ladder stile at the end of the track. The sight you behold must be one of the most stunning views in the country, let alone Derbyshire. In addition to the dale itself there is the old railway viaduct. Once thought of by some as a monstrosity and an unwelcome intrusion, it would now be difficult to imagine the dale without it.

Turn right along the path running above the dale. Stay on this to climb out on to the road to Monsal Head. Walk past the Monsal Head pub. At the crossroads, follow the signpost for Little Longstone and Great Longstone. This road descends through Little Longstone – with

34

Longstone Edge on the horizon to your left – passing the church on your left and a pinfold on your right. This old pinfold would have been used to keep stray cattle or sheep until they were collected by their owners, who would then have had to pay a fine to get their animals back.

Little Longtone displays an interesting variety of cottages on either side of the road. They were all built before the days of planning permission and yet blend in with each other in a way that modern properties often fail to do.

After passing the Packhorse Inn, walk past Home Farm and take the signposted path on the opposite side of the road for 'Ashford and Monsal Trail'. This leads slowly downhill to the lowest point of the field where it runs parallel to the wall. Climb over the stile and keep straight ahead through the next two fields. With the banking of the Monsal Trail (a disused railway line) to your right, walk 100 yards along the wall to the stile. Climb on to the Trail. Turn left along it, then, almost immediately, turn right off it. Cross the first field beyond the Trail. In the second field the path runs parallel to the wood on your left. If it is wet or damp, look out for the snails in this area. Instead of being the ordinary, yellow coloured snail with a vertical shell you may see some smaller, grey/brown wall snails, as they are known locally, with shells almost horizontal to their slippery little bodies.

At the end of the wood, the path carries on, before cutting across two narrow fields to the road. Cross the lane. The stiles on either side are full of fossils, but if you stand looking at them take care because the lane is narrow and the traffic can be fast. Walk along the left-hand side of the field the other side of the lane. Pass through the small gate and, keeping the wall on your left, walk behind the farm buildings on your right. It can be muddy here sometimes, but not impassable. Go through the squeezer stile and walk towards the stone outbuilding ahead. Proceed through the squeezer to the right of this structure and then along the narrow path to the road.

Cross to the steps leading up to the stile in the wall opposite and then walk across the field to the stile on the far side. This leads on to another road. Turn left and, ignoring the right turn into Highfields 150 yards or so further on, turn left again. Walk down the steepish hill towards the centre of Ashford. At the bottom of the hill, bear right towards the Ashford Hotel, 200 yards away. As you walk along the road to the hotel look out of a couple of wells regularly used for well dressings, on the left-hand side of the road.

8 Flagg
The Duke of York

Standing on the busy Buxton to Ashbourne road, the Duke of York is easy to find and popular with passers-by. As the nearest village is a mile or so away, it is clear this 15th century inn has been successful in meeting the needs of many thousands of travellers over the years. Despite its age the pub is surprisingly light. The bar in particular is cosy with beams and horse brasses, and the dining area is spacious. There is not much to see of the original features of the inn but it is good to see the present landlord is still intent on supplying good food and a welcome to match.

There is a wide range of meals and snacks to be had, for example, a 16 oz rump steak (for the hearty eater), a sausage sandwich, with side salad and chips, or a baked chicken breast. On Sunday the inn has a special licence which enables food to be served from noon to 9.30 pm. During the rest of the week lunch is available from 11.45 am to 2 pm and the evening meal from 6 pm to 9.30 pm. Robinson's traditional draught beer is sold, as well as Strongbow draught cider. There is a beer garden, a family room and a garden area for children.

Telephone: 0298 83345.

How to get there: The Duke of York is on the A515 about 5 miles south-east of Buxton.

Parking: While you walk you can usually park in the inn car park, subject to clearing this with the landlord. Otherwise, park at Earl Sterndale, and visit the Duke of York halfway round the circuit.

Length of the walk: 6¾ miles. Map: OS Outdoor Leisure 24 The Peak District/White Peak Area (GR 119675).

This is a circuit full of splendid scenery. Field paths and some road walking lead to impressive views near the hamlet of Crowdecote. From then on the walk passes through interesting and attractive countryside before making use of the High Peak Trail (a former railway line) to return to the inn. Take your OS map with you, if you can, as some of the paths are not obvious.

The Walk
From the pub, cross to Street Farm opposite. Climb over the stile at the side of the signpost. Avoiding the muckheap (as they call it in these parts), walk to the larger of the two gates in the far left corner of the yard. In the field beyond, walk down the right-hand side towards the bridge over the disused railway line. Cross the bridge and walk up the left-hand side of the field. At the top, pass through the gate and turn left towards the stile 20 yards away. Once over the stile, go alongside the wall in the next field and through the gateway – this can sometimes be muddy. Walk on the left-hand side of the wall in the next field, towards Hurdlow Grange ahead. Climb the stile (full of fossils) and walk directly across the field to the brightly painted stile.

Cross the small lane and scramble over the rather tumbledown stile at the signpost. Walk diagonally right to the gate in the top wall of the field and pass through it. Then walk towards a point 20 yards to the left of the far right corner of this field. This brings you to a flat track, formerly an old railway line. Walk round to the right of a dew pond. Bear half-right, slightly uphill, without gaining too much height. You need to pass through a gap in the wall to the right of a thorn tree in the field beyond. This wall runs to the right to join up with the old railway line.

After passing through the gap, walk down the right-hand side of the wall for the rest of the field, then the next field and then a third. At the end of the third, bear slightly away from the wall to walk down the right-hand side of a wood, after crossing a stile at the side of a pond. This leads to a stile on to the road.

Turn right and keep straight on at the crossroads, 300 yards away. The road then drops downhill. To the left is a splendid view down the

37

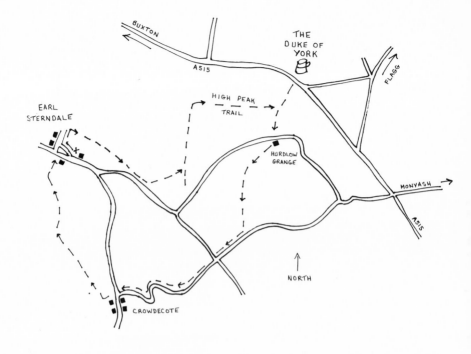

river Dove. Then, as you come to a second bend, looking up the valley, you see Parkhouse Hill and beyond that Chrome Hill, two very distinctive landmarks upstream. Take care on this stretch of walking, remembering not to walk on the inside of any bends. Continue walking downhill to the hamlet of Crowdecote.

About 80 yards before the Packhorse Inn, turn right along the road past Castle Way, then turn left, following the signpost for Glutton Bridge. Follow the track as it bears round to the right towards Meadow Farm. Stay on it as you pass through, with the farm on your left, and go straight on for 500 yards or so. Carry straight ahead where the wall bears right, towards the stile in front where a wall joins a fence. All the time you are heading towards Chrome and Parkhouse Hills. Walk up the right-hand side of the next field and over the stile towards a gravel track. Take the track which leads to the farm in front of you – ignore the footpath to the left. The prominent hill to the right is High Wheeldon, a National Trust property.

Pass through the gateway to walk directly through the farm. Stay on the track as you pass through gates and stiles until you come to a property known as Underhill. Take the stile on the right, then walk to the stile at the top of the field. Once over this keep straight on for

20 yards, then bear left along the path running uphill. Follow this until you come to a brightly waymarked stile at the top left corner of the field. Negotiate this and walk up the path on the right-hand side of the field. On your right is Earl Sterndale. Where the path levels out climb another colourful stile to the right. Walk down the field, climb another stile and head for the village. You are going towards the Quiet Woman pub. Look out for the stile to the left of the gate. Walk through the paddock behind the pub. Pass through a small gate at the side of the signpost for 'Crowdicote' (spelt differently from the OS map) and turn right in front of the pub. You will have some idea why the pub has its name when you see the sign on its wall that reads, 'Soft words turneth away wrath'.

Walk up beside the telephone box and turn left along the road in front of the church, then right at the side of the churchyard. Pass the playground and then, after the school, turn right along the tarmac lane, which becomes rougher as you progress. Stay on this for 400 yards, passing the houses and ignoring the rough track uphill to the left. The track brings you out on to a narrow lane. High Wheeldon looms in front of you like a grassy pyramid. Turn left and continue for about ⅓ mile until you come to a drive on your left. This leads up to Braemar Farm (Braemar House on the OS map).

About 100 yards beyond the drive, look for the steps in the roadside wall on your left. Climb these and bear half-right to the steps in the wall just above the gateway. From here continue in a straight line from the stile at the roadside to a third stile. Climb this and walk along the top side of a wall until you reach a green track. Follow this as it moves away from the wall and brings you to a fourth stile. The fifth stile in this sequence is in the far left corner of the next field. Once over this, head towards the two stiles in the trees to your right. Pass through both (no more than 10 yards apart). Bear slightly left to the wall on the far side of the field, which runs parallel to the trees you have come through. In the next field walk parallel to the wall to your left, towards a stile about 50 yards from the left-hand corner of the field. This leads on to a green lane. Turn left down this for 600 yards to its lowest point. On your right is the end of the High Peak Trail.

Turn right along this for ½ mile. The flowers are lovely here in springtime. After you have gone under the second bridge, turn left. Climb up the banking, over the stile and into the field. Return to Street Farm, walking up the left side of the field. Cross the farmyard and the road to reach the Duke of York.

Over Haddon
The Lathkil Hotel

The view from the Lathkil Hotel is one of the finest in England. One of the delights of walking in and around Lathkill Dale is to be able to sit in the window of the hotel afterwards and admire the countryside beyond – countryside that you will be able to enjoy on this walk. Ramblers are more than welcome in the hotel as long as they leave their muddy boots in their car or in the lower entrance.

The Lathkil is a freehouse and offers Wards and Darley real ales. The food is very popular, proving to be a draw to many people. The bar meals are tasty and varied and include lasagne, steak and kidney pie, a wide range of salads and some delectable sweets. Bar meals are available every day between noon and 2 pm. An à la carte menu only is on offer between 7 pm and 9 pm Monday to Saturday inclusive (no food on Sunday evenings). The landlord recommends booking for an evening meal.

Telephone: 0629 812501.

How to get there: Over Haddon lies just over 1½ miles to the south-west of Bakewell and is reached from the B5055 Monyash road. As you enter the village from Bakewell turn left just beyond the craft centre car park. The hotel is at the eastern end of the village.

Parking: There is a private car park behind the hotel as well as roadside parking in front. Customers are welcome to use the hotel car park if they wish to go for a walk. There is also a 'pay-and-display' car park at the other end of the village.

Length of the walk: 4½ miles. Map: OS Outdoor Leisure 24 The Peak District/White Peak Area (GR 207664).

Over Haddon stands on a hillside above the river Lathkill in an area mainly known for agriculture and, until a century ago, leadmining. This is a walk through a lovely area – typical Peak District scenery. Haddon Hall and Chatsworth House are within 5 miles of the village.

The Walk

Stand with your back to the Lathkil Hotel and admire the marvellous view. Turn left and climb through the stone stile 30 yards away. Take the right-hand path to walk through the next four fields with Lathkill Dale below to your right. The path is very clear on the ground. After crossing the stile into the fourth field, walk straight ahead to the farmgate on the far side of the field. Do not take the path going slightly downhill to the right.

Cross the road and climb the stile opposite. Walk towards the clump of trees in the far left corner of the next field and cross a stile. As you get nearer you will see some farm outbuildings amongst the trees. Go through the small bridlegate at the near corner of the trees and turn right immediately to walk between the farm buildings on your left and the trees on your right. It can be muddy. Continue down the metalled track, towards the hillside, surmounted by the TV transmitter, and the village of Alport. When you reach the road on the outskirts of Alport, cross it and take the lane opposite (to the left of a tall house).

After 80 yards you reach a small grass triangle in the road. The walk

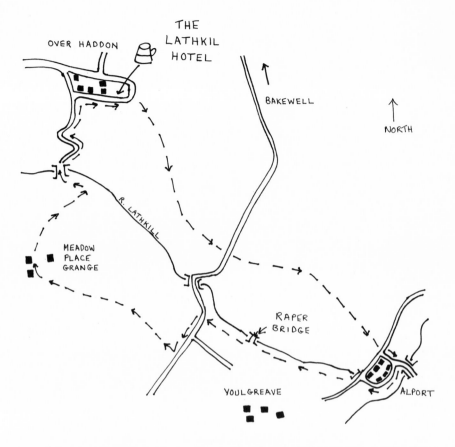

THE
LATHKIL
HOTEL

OVER HADDON

BAKEWELL

NORTH

R. LATHKILL

MEADOW
PLACE
GRANGE

RAPER
BRIDGE

YOULGREAVE

ALPORT

turns to the right here along the road in front of the houses. Take the
opportunity though to walk straight ahead to the bridge and admire
Alport Mill across the pond. There are usually fish waiting to be fed
under the bridge. Return to the grassy triangle and walk on through
Alport.

After passing Bradford Cottage on your right, cross the main road
and pass through the stile to the left of the metal gate. Walk up the
valley, keeping the fence and walls on your right. Just over ½ mile
later, walk past Raper Lodge on your left. This was featured in the film
of D.H. Lawrence's *The Virgin and the Gipsy.* Cross the narrow lane but,
before you pass through the stile opposite, turn right. This takes you
down to Raper Bridge, an old packhorse bridge in a beautiful setting.
There will be more hungry fish!

After returning to the stile, continue along the path up the valley
through three fields. When you reach the road turn left, uphill. Ignore

the road to Youlgreave to the left. Pass Glen Cottage and, 120 yards later, take the tarmac drive to Meadow Place Grange. The gate refers to 'Meadow Place'. This is an old road, not just a footpath. Keep on this for ⅔ mile and, 100 yards after passing through a pair of old, dressed gateposts, you come to the farmyard of the Grange. Turn right in the middle of the yard. Follow the waymarked route through two farmgates between the farm buildings. This brings you into the field beyond.

Cross the field, heading towards the far right-hand corner. You need, in fact, to aim for the gate 40 yards to the left of the corner. This leads you into the ash woodland of the Lathkill Dale National Nature Reserve. Follow the zig-zag track down into the dale bottom. Cross the river (if it is running) by the ancient clapper bridge. As the river Lathkill often runs underground at this point you may be able to cross the dry riverbed. The house in the valley bottom is Lathkill Lodge. Take the road running uphill to the right behind the Lodge. This zig-zags up into the village and is a steepish climb. Pass St Anne's church and fork right at the grass triangle. Walk through the village, mainly on the level, until you get back to the hotel at the far end.

Beeley
The Devonshire Arms

This popular pub is in the small village of Beeley, less than 2 miles south of Chatsworth House, the home of the Duke of Devonshire. Oak beams and, in winter, log fires welcome visitors to the pub, which was originally three cottages built in 1726. It was converted to an inn in 1746 and has quenched the thirst of many since then.

Meals are available from noon to 2 pm and 7 pm to 9 pm daily. As well as vegetarian meals and traditional food, the Devonshire Arms can be relied upon to come up with something different as well as tasty. The Cumberland sausage can be recommended and the haggis and neeps sound interesting, as do the smoked mackerel fillets with gooseberry chutney and the Stilton-stuffed pears with poppyseed dressing. There is usually a guest ale as well as Theakston XB, Old Peculier, Boddingtons and Marston's Pedigree. Try the Black Sheep if it is available. With draught cider, good food and a friendly atmosphere, the Devonshire Arms is well worth visiting.

Telephone: 0629 733259.

How to get there: Beeley is on the B6012 road, which joins the A6 and the A623. From the A6, head north from Rowsley, halfway between

Matlock and Bakewell, for just over a mile and take the first right into Beeley. The Devonshire Arms is straight in front of you.

Parking: You can park in front of the inn or across the road in the car park. There is an alternative parking place at Calton Lees car park in Chatsworth Park if you are unable to park in Beeley itself. To get there take the B6012 from Rowsley on the A6 passing the village of Beeley on the right. Two-thirds of a mile beyond Beeley cross the bridge over the river Derwent into Chatsworth Park. Then turn left 200 yards after crossing the bridge. The car park is ahead of you on the right-hand side of the road. If you start the walk from the Calton Lees car park walk along the road passing Chatsworth Garden Centre on your left. Proceed into the hamlet of Calton Lees and pick up the walk description from there.

Length of the walk: 6¼ miles, or 5½ miles if you take the shorter route back, omitting the climb up to Beeley Hilltop. Map: OS Outdoor Leisure 24 The Peak District/White Peak Area (GR 265675).

Chatsworth Park is one of the finest examples of parkland in England. Over half this walk is through the park and affords one or two marvellous views. The route runs alongside the Derwent for some distance, taking the walker right in front of Chatsworth House itself. There are only two climbs of any note – a gradual one from Calton Lees to Calton Houses and a steeper one up to Beeley Hilltop. This second one could be omitted, but a lovely view of Beeley and the valley beyond would also have to be forsaken.

The Walk
From the front of the Devonshire Arms, walk forward to the main road from Rowsley to Chatsworth. Turn right for 200 yards, passing the bus shelter. Opposite the church, turn left into the field by the signpost. Walk through the field along the straight path for ½ mile. Away to your left is the river Derwent. At the far end of this large field, turn left at the road and cross the bridge over the river. To your right is Chatsworth Park.

Once you pass the house on the left on the far side of the bridge, take one of the short paths up the bank in front of you, just before the road bends round to the right, and come out near to the entrance of Chatsworth Garden Centre on the left. Pass the entrance and turn left along the road signposted 'Chatsworth Forest Office and Sawmill'. Take no notice of the sign 'No thro' road' – this only applies to cars. You are now walking on a bridleway leading to Calton Lees.

Stay on the lane past the entrance to the sawmill on your left, as well as a sign saying 'Please hoot'! At the small grass triangle bear right

45

through the gate to walk along the track beside the hedge, with the stream on the other side. Walk on this track for ⅔ mile or so, slowly ascending to Calton Houses. Follow the track as it zig-zags up to the gate. It then passes between the houses. Go through the gateway at the end of the orchard, then bear right along the top side of the orchard and walk slowly uphill, looking back to your right down the valley you have just walked through.

At the end of the wall, in front of you, is Russian Cottage. The bridleway bears away from the wall to the left, towards a barn. After about 250 yards, the track passes through a gate in the wood to the left of this barn. Continue through the wood to a second gate – beyond this is a most beautiful view of Edensor (pronounced 'Enzer') and Chatsworth. Look out for the Emperor Fountain, sometimes visible to the right of Chatsworth House. Above the house is the Hunting Tower. In years gone by the ladies would watch their menfolk from this vantage point, hunting in the surrounding countryside. Next, walk along the path heading almost directly towards Edensor church in front of you, to the left of the small wood. Some of Chatsworth's deer may be around, so look out for these and, of course, keep your dog under control if you have one.

Once past the wood, do not follow the track down the hill, but keep straight on for the church, aiming directly for the spire. As you near the church, look out for the electricity sub-station on your left. Pass through the gate to the right of this and descend the steps into the village. Turn right and walk towards the church. John F. Kennedy's sister, Kathleen, is buried in the graveyard here. Her husband, Lord Hartington, brother of the present Duke, was killed during World War II. She subsequently died in an aircrash. The late president visited his sister's grave in 1963, amid great security.

Take the left-hand fork from below the church, towards the ornate gateway and on to the road. Cross this to the tree and seat opposite. Continue along the well-used path towards the trees. Once past these continue towards the House. When you arrive at the river bridge, but before you cross it, turn right across the meadow to the group of trees at the side of the river, 600 yards away. After ascending through the trees, bear round to the left and, after passing the weir next to the small plantation of conifers, keep straight on through the flat area beside the river. After passing a second weir, walk between the river and the ruin on the right. Continue towards the bridge. Go through the kissing-gate and turn left.

Once you have crossed the bridge, you can take the easy option and return to Beeley via the path across the field on your right – the way you came to the bridge on the outward route. However, an extra ½ mile or so (and a climb) can be added to the walk.

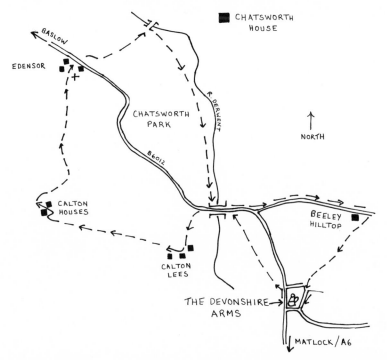

CHATSWORTH
HOUSE

BASLOW

EDENSOR

CHATSWORTH
PARK

R. DERWENT

B6012

NORTH

CALTON
HOUSES

BEELEY
HILLTOP

CALTON
LEES

THE DEVONSHIRE
ARMS

MATLOCK/A6

For the longer route, walk along the road away from the bridge. Keep on the left side of the road, taking care because of the traffic. As the road bears right after about 150 yards, take the left turn beyond the building on your left. This road is a dead-end for cars but not for walkers. Keep on this tarmac track as it climbs uphill. After passing buildings on your right (and the staddle stones – they look like stone mushrooms and were used to stack hay and corn on) take the right turn by the signpost. Pass through two squeezer stiles about 10 yards apart. At the entrance to the silage pit, follow the track round to the right behind the farmhouse. Pass through the gateway with the yellow waymark. Stay on the left of the field to the next gateway.

There is a lovely view of the valley and Beeley from this point. Walk on towards the village below and into the far corner of the field. Pass into the next field, walking straight ahead for the stile. After this stile, turn right down the field and proceed towards the stile in the bottom wall of the field, ignoring the stile in the wall on the left. Walk towards the far left-hand corner, along the hedge. When you have gone through the stile by the cottage, walk forward for 5 yards, then bear left along the road. Keep to the right of the tree in the grass triangle and walk downhill to the Devonshire Arms.

47

⑪ Hardwick Hall
The Hardwick Inn

This must be one of the few inns or pubs that have had a book written just about them. It is a fascinating place and Pamela Kettle's *A History of the Hardwick Inn* will give you all the details. According to the landlord, only about eight families have lived here in its 400 years. The inn stands roughly 600 yards away from Hardwick Hall, a National Trust property well worth exploring.

The number of people who use a pub is usually an indication of how good it is. The Hardwick Inn is always well frequented so you can draw your own conclusions. It offers both bar meals and a carvery menu plus blackboard specials and a children's menu. Besides standard items, such as 8 oz fillet steak with onion rings and mushrooms, prawn salad, and Stilton ploughman's, there are the specials, such as turkey stew or Barnsley chop. The carvery, too, offers a number of tempting options. Lunch is available at the usual times every day, and evening meals from either 6.30 pm or 7 pm to 9 pm each evening except Sunday (carvery closed all-day Monday and on Sunday evenings). Younger Scotch and Theakston XB are the real ales on sale and Autumn Gold and Dry Blackthorn the draught ciders. There are large lawns, ideal for children, three family rooms, and tables for eating at outside.

Telephone: 0246 850245.

How to get there: From junction 29 on the M1, take the Clay Cross exit. Then take the first left, signposted 'Stainsby and Hardwick Hall'. Continue along this road for the next 2½ miles, ignoring all further Hardwick Hall signs. Pass under the M1 and at the staggered crossroads ½ mile later, turn left for 200 yards to reach the inn.

Parking: Parking is available in the Hardwick Inn car park or, alternatively, park at Miller's Pond about ½ mile north-west of the inn and start the walk from there. Miller's Pond is the first turn left after passing under the M1 on your way from junction 29.

Length of the walk: 5¼ miles. Map: OS Pathfinder 779 Mansfield (North) and Part of Sherwood Forest (GR 459633).

This is not a particularly well known area for walkers drawn to the Peak District, but there is much to be discovered and explored. The route ventures across the border into 'foreign parts' – Nottinghamshire. Taking advantage of one of Derbyshire County Council's newer public footpaths (formerly a disused railway line) and marvellous National Trust property, this is an area worth seeking out. You can make a day of it by visiting Hardwick Hall afterwards.

The Walk

Stand in front of the Hardwick Inn with the pub behind you, then turn right through the gate with the 'No entry' signs. Walk up the driveway with Hardwick Hall above you to the left. After passing an old quarry on your left, the driveway turns sharply left. Leave the drive on the sharp left-hand bend and pass through the kissing-gate, heading through the field. As you walk along the quite well defined path, you pass a chimney on the left and then, at the end of the field, climb the stile to the left of the gate. Follow the track to the right alongside the fence. Bear slightly left before walking through the wood in front of you. The Hall is by now behind you to your left. Follow the well defined path through the wood. Where the wood extends to the left keep straight on towards the kissing-gate in the far right-hand corner. This path through the wood and across the field leading to it does not appear to be a public footpath as such. It is well walked, however, and there should be no difficulty in using it.

Pass through the kissing-gate onto the track and into the open. Walk down the track to the left for ⅓ mile, passing Far Paddock (a farm) on your left. Once you have passed The Old Granary and Norwood Lodge, follow the footpath shown by the signpost on your left. The path passes down the left-hand side of Norwood House. Take the path leading directly across the field, heading slightly left of the electricity pylon and houses in the distance. Once you are in the wood, go

49

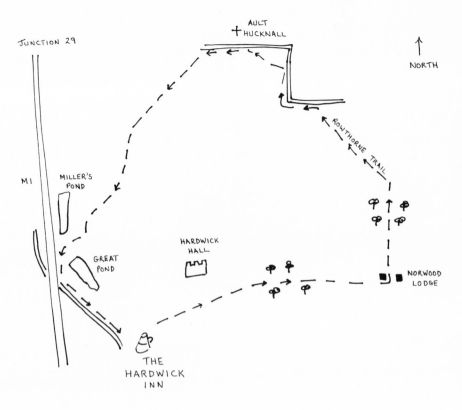

forward on the middle path, ignoring all side paths. This will bring
you to a footbridge which you should cross. Walk towards the far left-
hand corner of the field. At the disused railway line (the Rowthorne
Trail), turn left and walk along it towards the car park about ½ a mile
later. Like so many former railway lines the Rowthorne Trail has
quickly reverted to nature and birds can be heard singing in the trees
that line it.

Turn right at the car park and walk towards the road. Turn left and
then bear right at the tree in the middle of the road. About 250 yards
further along the road take the footpath indicated by the signpost on
the left. Walk towards the church on the hill in front of you, across
the two fields. You will see Bolsover Castle in the distance to the right.
Turn left at the road and pass the church on your right. It is usually
locked up, which is a pity.

Beyond the church, take the bridleway by the sign to the left. Stay
on this until you reach the lovely, unspoilt Grange on your right. Pass
through the white gate and walk to the right of Hardwick Hall in the

distance. At the end of the fence, bear slightly right towards the post in the field, just beyond the telegraph post. Walk parallel to the fence, past another post. Cross the tarmac drive before passing through the bridlegate and head towards the bridlegate in front of the pond. Turn right after the gate, down the track. This takes you past a quarry on your right towards the Miller's Pond car park and the M1.

Turn left along the road out of the car park and walk parallel to the motorway. Where the road disappears to the right under the motorway turn left. With the Hall on your left keep straight on, before bearing left at the sign for the Hardwick Inn. Take this road back to the pub.

Hardwick Hall is a National Trust property, built for Bess of Hardwick in the 16th century. It is a marvellous building standing on a hillside above the M1 and well worth exploring. The Hall is open from the beginning of April to the end of October on Wednesday, Thursday, Saturday and Sunday and Bank Holiday Monday from 12.30 pm to 5 pm (or sunset if earlier). To check opening times contact the Hall on 0246 850430.

⑫ Birchover
The Druid Inn

Many visitors to the Peak District will have heard of the Druid Inn, adjacent to Rowtor Rocks. Built about 225 years ago, it is a pub with a reputation for an excellent meal. This popular hostelry is likely to be very busy at weekends and holiday time, so choose the time when you visit. The inn has obviously been extended in recent years, mainly to cope with increased popularity. The oldest part of the inn, covered with a lovely creeper on the exterior wall, is cosy inside especially when the open fire is lit. Whilst in the village it is worth exploring the stone carvings in Rowtor Rocks. These were carved by the Reverend Thomas Eyre in the late 18th century.

Meals are served from noon until 2 pm and from 7 pm to 9.15 pm all week. There is no printed menu as such – everything is written on a large blackboard. The choice of dishes is usually varied and always delicious. Honey saddle of lamb baked with a sauce of redcurrant, gooseberry and mint, fruit and vegetable curry served on a bed of rice, mixed fruit and poppadum, cod and prawn bake with white wine and cheese sauce, Arabian lamb, potato, spices and butter beans, trout topped with prawn and mussels and white wine sauce – these are the sort of dishes you will find. For those who want

something simpler there are things like steak and potato pie, steak and mussel pie and steak and mushroom pie. The sweets are tasty too – for example, Bakewell pudding, apple and marzipan torte and also pecan and treacle tart. Real ale (Directors and a changing guest beer) and draught cider (Strongbow) are on sale. There is a terrace as well as a no-smoking area and a family room.
  Telephone: 0629 650302.

How to get there: Birchover lies between Bakewell and Matlock. Follow the B5056 south from the A6, between Rowsley and Bakewell. After approximately 2 miles, turn left uphill into Birchover. The Druid Inn is one of the first buildings on your right at the top of the hill as you enter the village.

Parking: You can use the car park by arrangement, while you walk, but there should also be space in the village street.

Length of the walk: 4¼ miles. Map: OS Outdoor Leisure 24 The Peak District/White Peak Area (GR 236621).

A typical Peak District walk with much of interest and good views. On the whole this is quite an easy route – nothing too strenuous. The Cat Stone and the Cork Stone as well as Rowtor Rocks make this a walk that children should enjoy.

The Walk
Walk down the track between the inn and the car park towards the church of St Michael and All Angels and the Old Vicarage. Next to the pond, where the track levels out, keep straight on, taking the right fork shortly after. You are heading towards the left-hand side of the rock outcrop (Robin Hood's Stride) on the other side of the valley. The rocky track becomes a grassy one. Where it forks again, bear slightly left uphill until you pass a tumbledown barn on the right. From here you have a good view of Robin Hood's Stride and the light-coloured track leading towards and then past it. This is the Portway, which is over 2,000 years old, an ancient route running from the Derby area into the Peak District.
  The track you are on is probably not quite so old. Your walk takes you round the bottom of the wooded hill on your left. So, at the end of the fir trees and just past the gateposts, bear left uphill, just before the section of track with the hawthorn along the right. Walk uphill alongside the wall, towards a stile at the side of the trees, about 50 yards from the track. Climb over the stile and keep ahead on the well defined path. To your right, across the valley, is Winster. Keep on past the ruin until you come to Rocking Stone Farm on your left over the

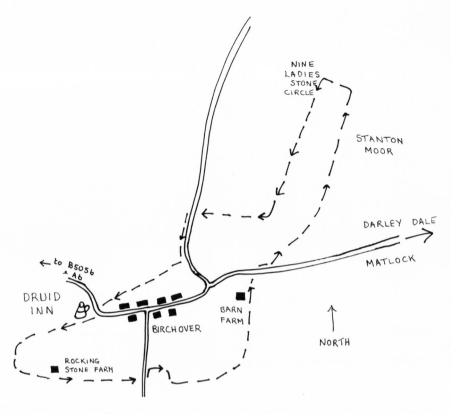

wall. At the corner of the garden (where the paths cross) keep straight on, with the wall on your left. Pass through the old gateposts and bear slightly right uphill. After passing through the step-over stile, walk along the right of the next two fields in the direction of the buildings in front. Birchover is now to your left.

When you come to the buildings you have been aiming for, take the stile at the gate to the right of the buildings and proceed along the track to the road. Turn left, then, less than 50 yards later, turn right at the small green triangle in the road – but not before looking at the old stocks a little further on. From the triangle, follow the track as it winds first right then left, passing Cowley Knoll Farm as you go. After passing another farm on your left, a few hundred yards later, walk alongside the first field on your left. Just beyond the end of this field, take the path through the stile at the side of the gate. With the hedge and wall to your left, carry on, ignoring all stiles on your left. In the second field, keep to the right of the muck heap. With the wall on

54

your left, walk on towards Barn Farm. Proceed around the right-hand side of the outbuildings, bearing left at the last one and walking straight ahead.

Go through the squeezer stile at the left of the last farm building and then the squeezer at the side of a gate just a few yards away. Walk up the right-hand side of the field to the road and moorland in front. At the road, turn right for 60 or 70 yards, then left at the sign 'Stanton Moor Stone Circle Ancient Monument'. Walk up the track for 100 yards and, where the tracks cross (the one from the left is not quite so distinct), take the track to the right, heading roughly in the direction of the rocky outcrop. This brings you to a National Trust sign for Stanton Moor Edge. Climb the stile over the fence and take the path to the left. Follow this fence and enjoy the views down the Derwent valley towards Matlock and Riber Castle in the distance.

The path does a 90 degree turn to the left towards a stone tower. On your right is the Cat Stone – a good place for a break, to take in the views from the edge of the Moor. Continue along the path towards the tower. This commemorates the mid 19th century Reform Bill and must command excellent views from the top – unfortunately, it is closed. Keeping on the path to the right and below the tower (ignoring the stile the other side of it), walk for another 200 yards. At this point cross the fence over the stile and, 10 yards later, turn left to the Nine Ladies Stone Circle directly in front of you – just beyond the circle is the King Stone. This Bronze Age circle is nowhere near as impressive or as large as Stonehenge (in fact, you may have difficulty spotting it initially) but it is approximately 3,500 years old and merits a bit of respect. Before you get to the stone circle, take the main path to the left, which cuts back across the top of the moor for the next ½ mile or so. You are now walking in the direction of Birchover again. When the track you are on begins to descend, follow the sandy track to the right, ascending slowly as you go. Stay on this until you come to another unusual rock rather like the Cat Stone. This one is the Cork Stone. Stay on the left of this and continue to the road.

Turn left at the road, passing Elizabeth Twyford's Quarry. Just beyond the buildings on your left, enter the informal car park on your right and walk directly away from the road towards the large boulders at the back of the car park. Pass between them and admire the view of Youlgreave in the middle distance and Over Haddon in the far distance. Take the path running left and passing the old building ruins, in a straight line (generally). Where there is a little kink in the path, keep straight on until you come out opposite the Druid Inn.

Ashover
The Red Lion Inn

13

The Red Lion stands 150 yards downhill from All Saints church. About a century ago, the pub that had been there for the previous 200 years was burnt down and the present pub, with its mock Tudor front, was built to replace it. Inside, the Red Lion is fairly spacious, with some interesting old photographs of the village and an impressive fireplace. Overnight accommodation is also available.

A lot of thought goes into the menu at the Red Lion. The landlord is keen to point out that he does not sell 'conveyor belt food', so you may have a wait – but it will be worth it. Besides bar snacks (scampi, roast chicken, hoagies, sandwiches and so on), there is also a grill menu, with such dishes as fillet and sirloin steak. Do look at the blackboard specials too. These change regularly, so you may not always be able to order smoked duck with mango coulis or beef dopiaza or cajun steak or mixed bean casserole. Rest assured, though, that the chef will come up with something just as tempting. The real ale on offer is Theakston Best Bitter. Food is available every evening from 7 pm to 9 pm and most lunchtimes from noon to 2 pm. Check opening times by telephone before you go.

Telephone: 0246 590271.

How to get there: Ashover is a mile to the east of the A632, which runs between Matlock and Chesterfield. Turn on to the B6036 at Kelstedge and follow this into Ashover. The Red Lion is on your right, downhill from the church.

Parking: You can use the Red Lion car park while you walk, but street parking is available nearby and is just as easy.

Length of the walk: 2½ miles. Map: OS Pathfinder 778 Bakewell and Matlock (GR 348630).

This is a short walk with plenty of interest. Ashover is 5 miles outside the Peak District but the scenery on the walk is as good as anything you will see in the National Park. All Saints church is worth looking round, as is 'Asher' itself. Take the opportunity to read something about its history on the board next to the Crispin Inn.

The Walk
Walk up the road from the Red Lion towards Ashover church and bear right along the road in front. After approximately 100 yards (opposite the Crispin Inn), turn right, along the track beside the rather grand building on the right, where an inscription refers to 'training a child'. Walk down the track, which soon becomes a path between a wall and a hedge. Pass the playing fields on your left. At the clubhouse at the far end, walk through the squeezer stile and keep on the distinct path ahead. The fields on the left are where Ashover Agricultural Show is held on the second Wednesday every year in August. Beyond these fields are the ivy-clad ruins of Eastwood Hall, bombarded by Roundheads during the Civil War and never repaired.

The path you are on should be easy to follow for the next five or six fields, walking in a straight line away from Ashover. Where the wall bears right, follow it all the way round to the stile by the gate. Once through this, walk parallel to the wood on your right. Cross to the stile leading into the wood. Follow the path through the trees for 150 yards. There is quite a drop on your right, into the quarry, so keep young children away from the fence.

At the end of the wood, turn right through the stile and walk alongside the wall on your left. The public footpath should pass between the rather tumbledown buildings on your left and the quarry hole on your right, but the path itself has slipped into the quarry. A diversion is in force, however, and you should follow this. It will lead back to the original line of the path, 30 or 40 yards away from a white house on your left. Pass through the squeezer stile to the right of the white house, then walk down the steps on to the road. Take great care

57

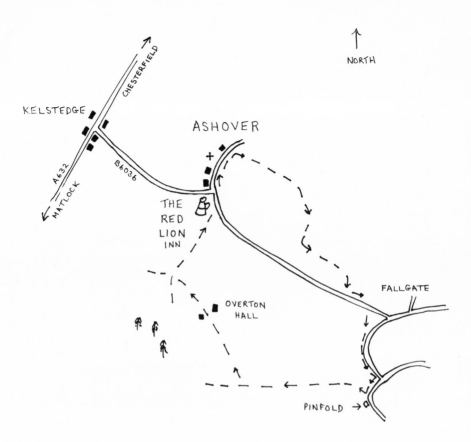

here – cars come quite fast from the right. Turn left along the road and, immediately past the house on your right (Green Bank), turn right down the driveway by the signpost. Keep down the left-hand side of the drive, firstly between the wall and the garage, then between the wall and the hedge. After crossing the small stream, continue to the road. Turn to the right, past the post and white rail fence. Stay on this road for 400 yards, with the river Amber on your right. After passing Wash Farm on the left, bear right over the road bridge, dated 1846. Continue forward, with the Miner's Arms on your right, towards the pinfold in front. Centuries ago stray sheep and cattle would be kept in the pinfold by a 'pinder' until their owners came and collected them, after paying a toll, of course. This is where the surname 'Pinder' originated.

From the pinfold, walk to the left of the Miner's Arms, passing down the track between the pub and Brookside Cottage next door. Proceed through the four grey posts. Ten yards beyond these the path forks.

Take the left fork, with the wall on your left. At the T-junction of paths, take the path up the steps on your left. On the right of the path is a working quarry. Continue until you come to a narrow field after 100 yards or so. Walk up the right-hand side of this field for 20 yards to the stile, then go through the right-hand side of the next field, through the gateway and on to the track at the side of the green metal signpost.

Ignoring the lane to the left and the rough path to your right, press forward on this track for approximately 350 yards, then turn right along the rough walled track. This leads to Overton Hall, 500 yards ahead. The Hall is now a residential home. As you walk up towards this old property, Cocking Tor is the wooded area to your left. You then pass Overton Park Camp. Stay on the track as you pass between Overton Hall on the right and Amber Lodge on the left. Just over 150 yards beyond these properties you reach a crossroads of tracks. Turn right along the track between the two lines of trees. Before you do this, look to your left along the path with old paving stones still in position. At the end of the trees, at the wall made up of stones standing on end, pass through the squeezer stile, after admiring the view of Ashover. Walk down the paved path in front (this can be slippery at times) and follow it downhill to the bridleway, which also continues downhill until levelling out. Bear left, and then right over the bridge over the river Amber. Climb up the bridleway and come out into the village beside the Red Lion.

14 Biggin-by-Hartington
The Waterloo Inn

The Waterloo Inn is a popular meeting (and eating) place with locals as well as walkers. The landlord of the Waterloo is keen to meet the needs of both. There are two rooms – a smallish one to the left and a larger one to the right. This is a typical Derbyshire pub, not centuries old but old enough to be appealing and attractive to those who want to be able to enjoy a drink or a meal in pleasant surroundings. Bar snacks and meals are available every lunchtime and early evening (except Christmas Day). Lunches are served from noon to 3 pm and evening meals from 6 pm to 9 pm, Sunday evening meals starting a little later, at 7 pm. The well-cooked meals provide good value for money. Cod in batter with tartare sauce, chips, side salad or peas, home-made lamb cobbler served with chips and vegetables, and Barnsley lamb chop served with side salad and chips or jacket potato give you some idea of the Waterloo's traditional approach. Three 'meals for tinies' are also offered and a high chair is available. The sweets are also reasonably priced and the ice-cream is particularly good. Besides the usual flavours, the Waterloo offers Drambuie, Tia Maria and honey flavours, and requests for double portions are the norm.

The meals are home cooked, the ale is real (Bass and Stones) and the welcome is warm. There is a no-smoking area, a beer garden, a family room and a garden area for children.
Telephone: 0298 84284.

How to get there: Biggin is 2 miles south-east of Hartington and can be reached from the B5054 or the A515 road, approximately 8 miles north of Ashbourne. The Waterloo is about 300 yards west of the church.

Parking: There is a reasonably sized car park at the front and side of the inn. Behind is a field which can be called into use quite easily. Ask permission though.

Length of the walk: 6½ miles. Map: OS Outdoor Leisure 24 The Peak District/White Peak Area (GR 152595).

This is a walk in the limestone area of the Peak District. The route passes through Biggin, Wolfscote and Beresford Dales. They are quite different in character but all were favourite haunts of Izaak Walton author of The Compleat Angler. *The three dales are understandably popular with walkers, particularly at weekends. If you want a more solitary stroll, go midweek.*

The Walk
From the Waterloo, turn left up the road towards the church. Immediately past the church turn right and walk along this straight road for 600 yards. Follow it to the right where it does a 90 degree turn. About 25 yards from the corner, go through the stone squeezer stile on the left and walk diagonally right to the stile 100 yards away across the field. Once through this stile, proceed to the right-hand side of the off-white house in front of you and walk through the brown gate between the outbuildings, on to the road. Turn left for 100 yards to the signpost. Follow the bridleway to the right into the dale, keeping to the right of the tumbledown wall.

The next mile or so of walking is through two lovely, grassy dales before you reach Dove Dale. After passing through a stile at the side of a gate, continue to descend gently – the dale opens out and is not so narrow as it was. Where the bridleway forks, with a small copse on the hillside above you to your right, take the left fork into Biggin Dale. At the National Trust sign, pass through the gate. The dale begins to change character now and there is a wood on your left. Still walking gently downhill, pass through a gateway. Two-thirds of the way down Biggin Dale, look out for a small cave on the left. Continue down the dale to the river Dove at Peaseland Rocks.

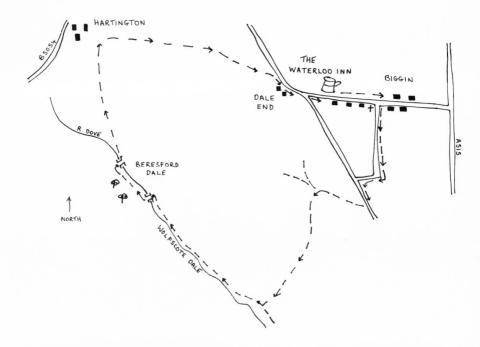

The scenery for the next 2 miles or so as you walk upstream beside the river Dove is Derbyshire at its best. Turn right into Wolfscote Dale and continue upriver, looking out for the birdlife, dippers in particular. These dark, dumpy birds, with a white 'bib' under their beaks, can be seen flying along the river or standing in it. Sometimes you may see them actually walking underwater as they forage for food amongst the stones. Over a mile from Peaseland Rocks, look out for a cave on the hillside to your right. Just beyond this cave you will come to a bridge crossing the river. Do not cross it, but head into the meadow beyond, keeping the river Dove on your left. At the end of the meadow, 300 yards away, cross the wooden footbridge over the Dove. Turn right into Beresford Dale, lush and narrow, which the path follows for the next 500 yards. The Dove is now on your right.

At Pike Pool, a lovely spot with a column of rock rising out of the water, cross over another footbridge on to the other side of the river. The path then climbs uphill, slightly away from the river, through trees. At the end of the clearing, the path leads into a field. Follow it straight ahead to the bottom side of a small hill in front of you. Go partway round this small hill and then walk ahead towards the two gateways, passing through the one on the right. Once through, turn half-right and head slightly uphill – the path is quite clear (though wide) at this point. The next stile is a squeezer in a tumbled down wall. Go through this and walk somewhat uphill to the right. Follow the waymarks to the track.

Turn right up this walled track to Crossland Sides (just a few farm buildings). Whilst walking up the track, take the opportunity to admire the view to the right towards Narrowdale Hill. At Crossland Sides the track joins a narrow country lane. Turn right, and then almost immediately left up another track. Where the track you are on joins another coming in from the left, turn right. After walking 15 yards or so climb over the stile into the long, narrow field stretching uphill away from the track. Some OS maps show the path at this point over the other side of the wall. This is not correct – you should walk on the left-hand side of the wall for 100 yards, then, 100 yards from the track, you must cross from the left-hand side of the wall to the right-hand side. Keep alongside the wall to the gate ahead.

Climb through the stile to the left of the gate. Then, keeping to the right of the small rock face (no more than 6 ft high) in the next field, climb the stile to the right of the rocks. Walk uphill, with the wall you have just climbed over on your left. At the end of this wall, keep straight on across the open field to the stile 75 yards in front. This leads into a large field. Cross this field to the gate in its corner, diagonally opposite.

After passing through the gate, walk along the walled track to the right for ½ mile or so, ignoring the tracks to left and right. Eventually you will come out to the road at Dale End. Turn right at the road and, 150 yards later, take the left fork and follow the road back into Biggin village and the Waterloo.

15 Parwich
The Sycamore Inn

Parwich is full of character (and stone cottages) and is at the centre of the White Peak area, the limestone part of the Peak District. All outward appearances suggest Parwich is a quiet, sleepy village, but you do not have to delve far for evidence to suggest otherwise. The local church is thriving and there are clubs and other groups meeting on a regular basis. This is how a village should be: full of community activity and care.

Ramblers, walkers, hikers – call them what you will – they are all welcome at the Sycamore, a cosy pub built in Derbyshire stone. The rooms are snug and there is a friendly, easy-going atmosphere. The meals are served from noon to 2 pm and from 7 pm to 9 pm (except Sunday evenings). You can have the choice of soup and roll, 6 oz sirloin steak, sausage and egg, trout, large filled Yorkshire pudding and omelettes with various fillings, amongst other things. There is also a children's menu. The real ale is Robinson's Best Bitter and Best Mild and Strongbow Dry Cider is on offer too. There is a beer garden and a family room and children are welcome.

Telephone: 0335 25212.

How to get there: Parwich is about 5 miles due north of Ashbourne and is reached from the A515 Buxton road. The Sycamore Inn is no more than 100 yards from St Peter's church.

Parking: Feel free to use the car park while you walk. Either ask permission first or leave a note under the windscreen to let the landlord know what you are doing. There is parking in the streets nearby, in any case.

Length of the walk: 4¼ miles. Map: OS Outdoor Leisure 24 The Peak District/White Peak Area (GR 188543).

This walk between the attractive villages of Parwich and Tissington has wide views across the surrounding countryside. Both villages are popular with tourists, especially Tissington, and each community boasts an ancient church. You will walk into, and then out of, the valley of Bletch Brook twice, so allow plenty of time to stop and enjoy the scenery as you go.

The Walk

From the Sycamore, turn right towards the small green beside the church. Follow the road as it bears round to the left. Ignore the road to the left to Alsop-en-le-Dale and keep straight on. Where the road bears right to Newhaven and Buxton, walk forward, with the shop on your left, towards the clock on the school building. Turn left beside the school and then, a little further uphill, right at the signpost to follow the path through the fields. This is a straight path with clear stiles. About 400 yards later you come out on to a narrow country lane. Cross this and pass through the stile opposite. Walk up the right-hand side of the field to a sunken lane (sometimes boggy or overgrown), 70 yards later. Once you have got to the top, turn right along the track and, 75 yards later, turn left when you reach a field. Stay on the left side of this and the next field. At the start of the third field, bear diagonally right to a footbridge. Once over this, walk left to another footbridge in the marshy valley bottom. This is a quiet, peaceful place, worth enjoying if you want a rest before climbing out of the valley.

Head straight up the middle of the field from the bridge. After passing through the broken line of hawthorns, zig-zag up to the top left-hand corner of the field. Pass through a gate. Then bear half-right towards the Tissington Trail. This is a disused railway line which is obscured until you are above it, as this section is in a cutting. It has now been designated a public right of way. As you walk up the field towards the Trail, there is a lovely view up the valley towards the small village of Alsop-en-le-Dale. Cross the stone bridge over the Trail

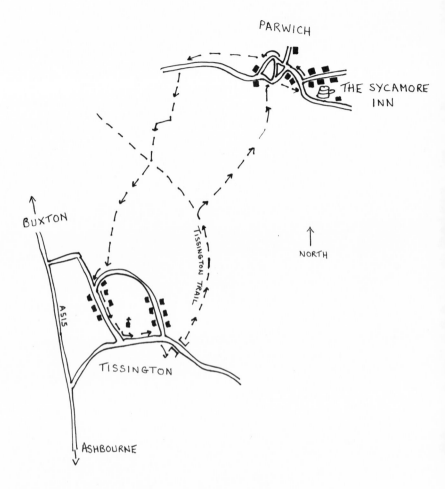

to walk through the ruins of Crakelow Farm.

Leave the farmyard by the track. Where the ground levels out, keep straight on towards the stile, 60 or 70 yards left of the gate. Follow the path in the next field, walking parallel to the wall on your right towards the stile ahead. Keep straight on towards Tissington through the next three fields. Keep the wall on your left in the first one and then on your right in the next two. This should bring you to a very short walled path past a cottage on your right.

Turn right into the village. Pass the sub post office and walk down the road to the left, descending gradually to the grass triangle at the bottom of the village. On the way you pass Tissington Hall on your right and St Mary's church on the left. The church is usually open and warrants a walk round. At the grass triangle, turn left to walk past the pond on your right, before bearing right along the road. Turn right down the track to the car park (and toilets) on the Tissington Trail.

Tissington is one of the Derbyshire villages that annually (near Ascension Day) organises a well-dressing ceremony, the centuries-old custom dating back to pagan times when thanks were given to the water god for keeping the wells running. You will have passed a number of wells as you walked through the village.

Once you have descended to the Trail, turn left under the bridge. This brings you into the Tissington Station Cutting Nature Reserve, a Derbyshire Wildlife Trust area. Stay on the Trail, ignoring the path that crosses it after a few hundred yards – to the right to Bradbourne and to the left to Tissington. At the end of the nature reserve, the Trail opens out, with good views to your right towards Parwich. Beyond Parwich (on the far horizon) is a small group of trees. This is Minninglow, a Neolithic burial chamber. To the right, the masts of Alport Heights can sometimes be seen 8 miles away.

Before you get to the next bridge, with an old stone barn to its left, turn left off the Trail on to the path. Walk up the steps, following the sign stating 'Footpath to Tissington and Parwich'. Turn right and cross the bridge. Follow the track as it bears left. At the footpath signpost, turn right, following the line of the signpost. Pass through a stile and continue straight ahead to pass through the squeezer stile. In the flat valley bottom, continue ahead towards the footbridge over Bletch Brook. Once across, bear slightly left uphill until you reach a rather unusual stile/bridge, with no water underneath.

Walk down the left side of the next two fields. Parwich lies in front of you with Parwich Hill behind. After passing through the squeezer stile at the end of the second field, bear left towards a stile, just uphill from the gate in the bottom left-hand corner. Walk to the left of the red-brick chimney and then towards the road. On reaching the signpost marked 'Tissington 2', turn right to the squeezer stile. Follow this almost tunnel-like path alongside the small brook, which may be dry in summer. It provides welcome shade on a hot day. After 150 yards keep straight on as the path becomes a track, to reach the road and return to the Sycamore Inn.

Brassington
The Olde Gate Inne

If you are a lover of traditional English pubs do visit the Olde Gate Inne. It is the oldest building (but one) in the attractive village of Brassington and is full of character and oak beams. It was built in 1616 and some of the timber is from ships sunk at the time of the Spanish Armada. The haunted dining-room was a makeshift hospital during the Civil War. You really need to visit it to appreciate its character.

The landlord is proud to make it clear that there are no chips sold at the Gate. On a Sunday there is a traditional Sunday roast but, otherwise, he is keen to try and give you something different – for instance, spinach and mushroom lasagne, vegetable casserole, salmon and broccoli fettuccine, steak and venison casserole and pheasant. Barbecued food is also on offer during the summer and curries in winter. Lunch is served from noon to 1.45 pm (Monday to Friday) and noon to 2 pm (Saturday and Sunday). Evening meals are available daily, except Mondays, from 7 pm to 9 pm, sometimes different in winter. Marston's Pedigree is available with Owd Roger and Merrie Monk in winter. Draught cider, Strongbow and Woodpecker, can be had and use can be made of the beer garden in good weather.

Telephone: 0629 85448.

How to get there: Brassington lies on a minor road between Matlock and Ashbourne and can be reached from the B5035 or the B5056. The Olde Gate Inne is 100 yards or so along the road from the church.

Parking: If you want to use the pub car park while you walk, contact the landlord first. As an alternative, there is usually room to park in the village streets.

Length of the walk: 4½ miles. Map: OS Outdoor Leisure 24 The Peak District/White Peak Area (GR 230543).

A fairly easy walk with a chance to visit Harboro' Rocks and, further on, a particularly good view from Carsington Pasture over Carsington Water. Part of the route is on a section of the High Peak Trail.

The Walk
Stand with your back to the Gate and turn right along the road below the church. Keep on this road, with the church and graveyard on your left. At the end of the churchyard, turn left up the road past Coach House and Honeysuckle Cottage. Immediately beyond the latter, take the gennel winding uphill. Where it joins the other small lane, turn right at Dale Cottage down to the main road. On your left at this point is Brassington village hall (formerly a church). Walk up the road past it and, 100 yards later at the 'dead end' signpost, turn right along the tarmac lane.

Walk along this lane past the old quarry and where it ends, 400 yards beyond the quarry, climb into the field on the left, following the footpath marked by the signpost. Walk alongside the fence for the next 500 yards – this will involve a 90 degree right-hand turn, followed by a 90 degree left-hand turn, before you reach the next road. The field you walk through is full of the old lead workings typical of the area.

At the road turn right and continue, passing on your left a works site with Harboro' Rocks behind. About 100 yards beyond the entrance, take the footpath to the left and follow it along the track towards the High Peak Trail and Harboro' Rocks.

If you want to take a closer look at Harboro' Rocks take the footpath opposite the point where you join the High Peak Trail.

Turn right along the Trail for just over ½ mile. The High Peak Trail was formerly the route of the Cromford and High Peak Railway, which ran from the Cromford Canal towards Buxton, 17 miles away. It was mainly used for industrial purposes, although at one time passengers were carried. Constructed in the 1820s, it lasted just over 140 years

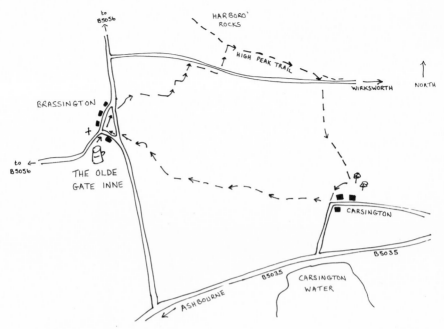

before being closed. A few years later the rails were removed and the Trail was born.

At the derelict buildings, take the short footpath to the right to the road, leaving the Trail at the signpost for Carsington. Cross over the road and climb the stile into the large field beyond. Note the remains of an old windmill to your left. Keeping the wall on your left for the next ⅔ mile, walk on until you reach the wood above Carsington village. Marvellous views of the village and Carsington Water open out in front of you.

Head partway down the side of the wood before walking half-right downhill towards the highest cottage on the hillside. There is a little gate to the left of this cottage. Pass through this and walk down the path to the road. Turn right up the road marked 'cul-de-sac'. Keep on this track for 250 yards, climbing uphill, to the end of the houses. Pass through the gate at the signpost for Brassington. Keep on the track for the next 600 yards, with a stone wall on your left for the last 350 yards. Pass through the stile at the left of the gate and head straight on along the slightly sunken path. Do not follow the track to the left from the gate.

Keep straight ahead to a small pond. Cross the stile to the side of this pond and cut across the corner of the field to another stile, approximately 50 yards away. Bear slightly right downhill. There is a

70

reasonably clear path with a stile at the bottom of the field. Once through this, bear slightly right to the stile, 25 yards to the left of the building in the far corner. Cross the track and pass through the stile to the right of the gate. Follow the track for just over 150 yards and just after it has levelled out (but before it starts to rise again), leave it and take the reasonably well defined path to the left of a small wall. This becomes clearer to follow, passing between the hummocks. Brassington emerges ahead of you.

Continue on the path between the hummocks to the stone squeezer stile. After passing through, walk on with the wall on your left, looking out for a stone stile. Go through this and walk down the right-hand side of the field. Halfway down this wall (after 100 yards), go through the stile. Head slightly left to the stile on the other side of the field. Pass through and continue to the far left-hand corner of the next field. Climb up the steps, going through the stile and into the farmyard. Keeping the wall on your left and the breeze-block buildings on your right, proceed through the farmyard to the road and the village.

Once on the road, cross over and then head uphill to the Miner's Arms ahead of you. Keep on this road, bearing round to the left, until you return to the Olde Gate Inne.

Winster
The Miners' Standard

Perched on the hillside above Winster, this 17th century, oak-beamed pub is full of character and interest. There is, for example, a fascinating collection of minerals. The name of the pub derives from the dish that local leadminers used for measuring ore – the dish was the miners' 'standard'.

The 'standard' of the excellent-value food is good too. You will find dishes such as steak and kidney pie, a delicious chicken, leek and ham pie, Cumberland sausage ring and egg and chips – mainly home-made and all definitely tasty. Meals are served from noon to 1.45 pm every day and in the evenings from 7 pm to 9 pm Thursday and Friday, 7 pm to 9.30 pm Saturday and 7 pm to 8.30 pm Sunday. Lunches only, on the other days. There is also a restaurant, a beer garden and an outside area for children. The real ales are Marston's Pedigree, Boddingtons and Black Sheep, and draught cider is also sold.

Telephone: 0629 650279.

How to get there: The Miners' Standard lies on the B5056, which links the A6 south of Bakewell with Ashbourne, and is at the south-western side of the village of Winster.

72

Parking: There are two car parks, either of which you can use while you walk, if you ask first. Alternatively, park near the green opposite or on the road beyond the green.

Length of the walk: 2¾ miles. Map: OS Outdoor Leisure 24 The Peak District/White Peak Area (GR 238602).

Winster is full of attractive houses and there are gennels to explore. The circuit, which is mainly over fields and along tracks, includes some easy-going ascents affording lovely views.

The Walk
Walk uphill from the Miners' Standard, then take the road on the right, signposted 'Elton 1½ – Newhaven 4½'. About 100 yards along this road, turn right again along the rough track, marked 'Limestone Way'. This is Islington Lane. Where it forks, keep right. You soon pass Grey Tor, an outcrop of rocks on the right, surmounted by trees. The track descends to cross a farm drive. Turn right to go down gradually along the drive, ignoring the footpath across a field on your right. The drive zig-zags to the road. Cross over to Water Lane, the narrow green lane opposite. This leads you to Winster cemetery.

Once out on to the road, turn right towards the village. Just 20 yards later, though, cross the road and walk down another track towards the trees. This track (Placket Lane) divides just over 200 yards from the road. Take the right fork, which descends very slightly before bearing right. Stay on the track until just before it rises. At this point, take the path to the left, which starts to climb through the trees and brings you to a stile. Pass through this into a field. Turn right to another stile nearby. Walk up the field from this second stile, towards the outbuilding ahead. Stay just to the left of this, but to the right of the farm buildings immediately beyond. Pass through the stile at the side of the outbuildings.

About 30 yards down the track, follow the narrow path through the squeezer stile. This leads, between walls, to Main Street, Winster. The village is full of interesting buildings and you have the opportunity to see some as you turn left along the street. After passing Winster Hall, built in 1628, on the left, in front is the red-brick Market Hall. This is one of the smallest National Trust properties and it was also the first in Derbyshire. Turn right in front of the Market Hall to walk up East Bank. Pass the Bowling Green pub on your left and then the Wesleyan Reform church on your right. Where the road forks, take the left-hand one and, 75 yards later where the road bears right, you must turn left to look for a public footpath signpost, pointing along the path between the walls of Headlands Cottage and Walton Cottage. The path

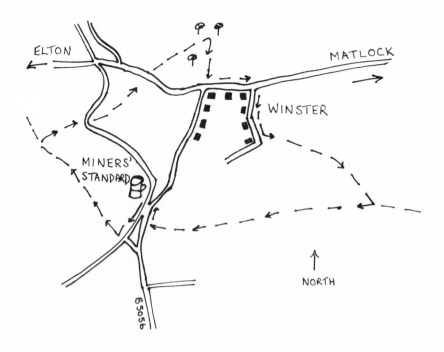

then runs above a garden on your left to a squeezer stile.

Continue straight on through the first field, then walk diagonally right in the next field towards the trees. After passing through a waymarked old stile, bear left and continue forward through the next four fields. Look out for the gritstone squeezer stile. From here walk towards the fir trees in the rocks 120 yards or so ahead. Only 40 yards or so into the field, however, the path reaches an 'elbow' of wall (on your left), jutting out into the field. Once you reach this point, bear back to your right at an acute angle to the top right-hand corner of the field. This brings you to a track, which you follow to the right for the next ½ mile.

On your way you will see a most unusual seat, presumably designed and constructed locally. There is no indication who put it here. It affords good views over the village of Winster below, towards Stanton Moor and Birchover beyond. As you reach the road the ground on your left is commonland and beyond this is Mosey Mere. This used to supply water to the small village of Islington Green. Opposite is a lead ore house. Rather like using a modern nightsafe, local leadminers used to store their ore in here until 50 years or so ago. From here, walk down the road back to the Miners' Standard.

18 Bonsall
The Barley Mow

The Barley Mow in Bonsall is worth passing a few other pubs for. This one-room hostelry, with its pleasant sun terrace at the front, has an easy-going atmosphere and friendly staff, and serves excellent home-cooked food at reasonable prices. The landlord is (at the time of writing) an Environmental Health Officer, so you will expect a clean and spotless pub – and that is what you get. A possible added bonus is that he organises his own walks. After you have done this one, have a word with him if you like the idea of another local (4 mile) guided walk from the pub and back in time for lunch. You must also ask him to tell you something about hen racing.

Cauliflower cheese, cottage pie, beef pie, scampi and gammon are examples of the staple dishes on offer. Then there are specials (which change regularly), for instance, liver and onions, braised steak and curry with rice or chips. The real ale is Kimberley Classic and there is an occasional guest beer. If you want to take your children, they are welcome before 9 pm, and there is a tailor-made children's menu. Opening times are evenings only during the week (6 pm to 11 pm), on Saturday from noon to 11 pm and on Sunday from noon to 3 pm and then from 7 pm to 10.30 pm. Finally, quite an unusual service is offered. Whilst dogs are not allowed in the pub, dog-sitting is available at an hourly rate.

Telephone: 0629 825685.

How to get there: Bonsall is 1½ miles from Cromford, south of Matlock. Turn off the A6 in Cromford as though you are heading towards Wirksworth and, in less than 200 yards, turn right past the Greyhound pub on the right. Follow the A5012 (the Via Gellia) for just under a mile until you see The Pig O' Lead on your right. Turn right up the hill to the right of the pub and stay on this road into Bonsall village. Take the second left ½ mile after The Pig O' Lead, at the stone monument in the road. The Barley Mow is 400 yards later on the right.

Parking: There is no objection to you parking in the car park while you walk. Alternatively, parking is possible in the streets of Bonsall.

Length of the walk: 3¾ miles. Map: OS Outdoor Leisure 24 The Peak District/White Peak Area (GR 275580).

This walk takes you up and down, over hillsides, along tracks and through woodland. The area is full of interest and there are some splendid views, particularly of Matlock and the Derwent valley, and the famous limestone rockface of High Tor.

The Walk
From the Barley Mow, walk down the road with the pub car park on your right. Stay on this road for 400 yards or so until you come to the unusual stone structure in the middle of the road. Keeping to the left of this, pass through the stile into the grassy playground beyond, then turn left to walk up the steps leading towards the church of St James above. Go through the churchyard, keeping the church itself on your right. When you come to the lychgate beyond the church, turn right up the road towards the school. Only 20 or 30 yards later ascend the lane to the left, passing the house called 'Torber'. Keep on this sunken lane (known as Ember Lane) as it climbs uphill, until it levels out. Over 2 miles away, to the right, can be seen the tower known as Crich Stand, a memorial to soldiers of the Worcestershire and Sherwood Foresters Regiment.

Approximately ½ mile after leaving the church, you come to Ember Farm on the left. Keep straight ahead on the lane through the gateway and, 50 yards later, bear left to the signpost for Matlock. Ignore the path downhill to the right of the signpost. Walk straight ahead along the clearly defined path through the trees and, later, into the deciduous woodland. The wood at this point is full of beech trees. The path leads across this wooded hillside with a steep drop away to your right – keep your eyes on the path!

Ahead you see signs of the terminal buildings of the Heights of Abraham and the cable car. Approximately 100 yards before the grounds of the Heights of Abraham, take the left-hand fork in the path,

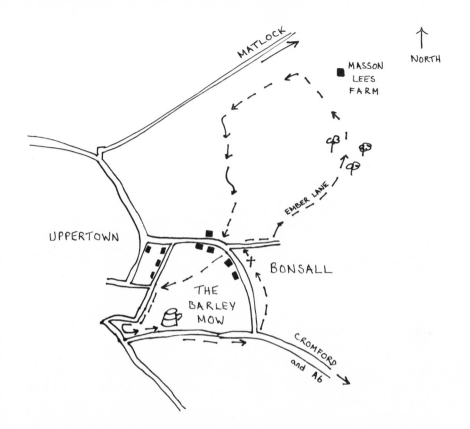

climbing slightly uphill through the trees. Pass through the squeezer stile at the edge of the wood. Bear right downhill towards High Tor on the opposite side of the Derwent valley below you. This famous local landmark rises nearly 400 ft from top to bottom and is usually viewed from the A6. From this viewpoint it looks quite different. The limestone rockface is very popular with climbers and they can often be seen hanging precariously above the river Derwent. To gain access to the grounds behind High Tor an entrance fee is payable.

At the bottom of this field, in front of the white gate, turn along the level path to the left. Walk parallel to the wall on the well defined path. Go through the small gateway, which leads to some old workings. Beyond these, climb slightly uphill, passing a mineshaft covered by concrete sleepers. The whole of this hillside is riddled with these old mineshafts – stay clear of them, they can be dangerous. Keep straight ahead through the brambles and thorns (ignoring the green arrows) until the path joins a gravel track. Turn right on this, walking downhill along the bottom side of a number of fields. Matlock can be seen in the valley below. Keep on the track as it descends and subsequently ascends. Down the hillside to your right is Masson Lees Farm. Eventually the track levels out and you come to 'Geoff's Seat' (erected in memory of a local Matlock solicitor) on your left. There are marvellous views of Matlock and the Derwent valley from here. Feel free to use the seat and admire the scenery.

Only a yard or so beyond the seat, turn left and walk diagonally uphill away from it. You will come to a gap stile. Keep straight ahead for 30 yards, then cross the wall on the right and cut across the corner of the field to another stile. This brings you out on to a stony track descending to your right. Cross this to the stile opposite and walk on through the narrow field and into the next (narrow) field. At the far end of this field go through the gap and head across the corner of the field to a signpost and a stile in the hedge. Turn left once you have gone through the stile and follow the track, staying on it between the hawthorns. To your right (across the valley) is Uppertown, Bonsall. The grassy track you are on descends to a gate. Pass through it and follow this walled path down the hillside. Shortly after the gate, take the left fork in the path. Ignore all paths off to the right. It eventually levels out, with open views of Bonsall to your right.

This walled path joins a track with a concrete surface. Take this down to the right, coming out at Bonsall Cross. Go straight across the road, with the King's Head on your left. You need to find the footpath bearing to the right of the breeze block walls – about 30 yards from the road you should see some steps. Follow these for 200 yards as the path climbs between walls away from Bonsall. When it crosses the narrow field, take the right-hand stile in front, ignoring the one to the left. The stile you want leads you onto another low-walled path. Follow this all the way to Uppertown, passing some unusual rocks in the garden walls. At the road, turn left to go down Bankside. Follow this down until it comes to the Bonsall Ebenezer Wesleyan Reform Chapel, dated 1893. As you descend Bankside you will see – just past Annadale but before the road disappears round a right-hand bend – a short-cut down a little tarmac path to the left. This short-cut misses out a sharp bend in the road and brings you back to the road which then leads down to the chapel. With the chapel on your right, take the left fork. Stay on this road, ignoring any turning to the right, as it descends to the Barley Mow.

19 Tansley
The Tavern

Previously known as the George and Dragon, the Tavern shed its old name a few years ago. The metamorphosis has resulted in the pub going up-market, though not so far as to be unwilling to serve walkers. The Tavern has, in fact, come a long way from its origins as a farmhouse, when ale was served from the farm kitchen. The restaurant at the Tavern was originally the cowshed.

The food here is very good and the Tavern is well worth visiting. There is a standard menu with different specials daily, except on Sunday when a traditional lunch is served. Giant Yorkshire puddings with different fillings (steak and kidney or chilli or vegetable curry) are a favourite. Home-carved gammon with egg or pineapple is another. Then there are the more usual items, like fillet or sirloin steak, mixed grill, and a range of vegetarian and children's dishes. Food is served daily from noon until 2 pm and from 6.30 pm until 9 pm (evening meals starting at 7 pm on a Sunday). There is a choice of real ales – either Ind Coope Burton Ale or Tetley Bitter. Strongbow draught cider is also available. There is a beer garden in front of the Tavern.

Telephone: 0629 57735.

How to get there: One of the easier pubs to find, the Tavern at Tansley lies on the A615 Alfreton road, 2 miles from Matlock.

Parking: The car park is opposite the pub. The owners have no objection to you using it, while you walk, but it is courteous to ask first.

Length of the walk: 3 ¼ miles. Map: OS Outdoor Leisure 24 The Peak District/White Peak Area (GR 324595).

A short walk through what remains of one of the oldest industrial valleys in this country. Thanks to The Arkwright Society, old mills and dams in danger of falling into disrepair have been made safe. There is one uphill section out of Tansley (up Oaksedge Lane), giving you a good excuse to stop at the top to take in the view of Riber Castle and the surrounding countryside.

The Walk
Facing the Tavern, with its car park behind you, walk along the road to the right of the pub. This is signed 'Unsuitable for Heavy Vehicles'. This road bears left into Church Street. At the T-junction, turn right, rising slightly as you pass the Methodist church, the community hall and Tansley House. Then walk past the church and the village hall.

At the end of the children's grass playing field, turn left into The Knoll. Follow it as it bears right for 400 yards, passing the entrance to Riber View Close and also the signpost for Lumsdale and Matlock. At the T-junction, turn left on the road going downhill, and cross the stream. Bear right uphill and stay on this lane as it begins to rise quite steeply. About 350 yards later you will walk by Oak Edge Lodge (this is shown as Oak Edge Farm on the OS map) – by now the lane is a sandy track rather than tarmac. This levels out and, just before it descends, turn half-right by the gatepost along the well defined path leading into the bracken and trees. Stay on this footpath as it meanders between the silver birches. After 150 yards it levels out and runs straight ahead along a bank side through trees, with the ground falling away to your left. The path then forks, going uphill to the right and downhill to the left. Take the left fork. Follow the path as it meanders over the next few yards in the pine woodland, until you stand on a small hillock. From here there are good views of the outskirts of Matlock and the pond which you will pass later.

Continue along this uneven path through the bracken (or ferns, depending on the time of year), with the pine trees on the bank to your right. The path eventually runs along beside a wall for 30 yards. Follow this round to the left, then, 50 yards later, take the right-hand path. With fields on your right, you will see on the left what remains

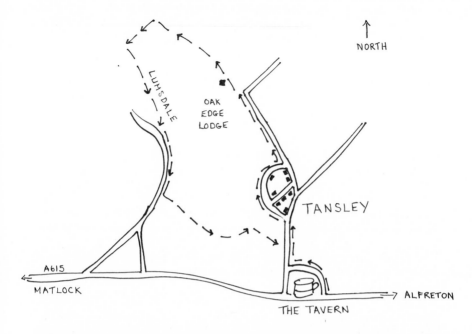

of a centuries-old millpond in what is, perhaps surprisingly, one of the oldest industrial valleys in England. This particular area was also once a rubbish dump and there are many signs that diggers have been looking for old bottles and other finds. At the end of the path, cross the footbridge and walk out onto the road until the local comprehensive school (Highfields) is in front of you.

Turn left down the road past Ivy Cottage. Where it bends right, keep straight on along the rough track. Now on your left is the millpond, seen from the other side. At the end of this silted up pond you can see traces of the dam wall. In the grass below the old pond are the ruins of a bone mill. Keep on down the track by Beech House on your right and pass another silted up millpond on your left. Go by the row of cottages to the left and come out at another pond, full of water this time. Walk down the right-hand side of this pond – alongside it rather than on the track to the right. At the end, follow the path downhill that leads through the ruins of the old mill buildings. Ensure that Bentley Brook is no more than 10 or 15 yards away on your left as it tumbles, sometimes spectacularly, down the valley.

These ruins have been cleared in recent years by the Arkwright Society, a charity based at Cromford Mill, south of Matlock. The society's efforts are directed, in particular, towards the 'practical conservation of industrial monuments'. It is always looking for support, both practical and financial. Call at Cromford Mill if you are interested.

At the end of the largest ruin (on the bank above the red-slated buildings), turn left and follow the steps downhill, with the stream still no more than 10 or 15 yards away on your left. Turn left at the road, taking care as you go. Follow the road for 500 yards down the valley, ignoring the path to the left and the one to the right. You will notice by now that Bentley Brook is on your right. Pass through the Lumsdale Mill complex on the road. Then 100 yards beyond the entrance to Tansley Wood House, where the road bears right, walk forward along the track. There is a small muddy pond on your left where you leave the road.

Stay on the track until it becomes a tarmac path through a field. It then passes along the top side of a wood. At the end of this wood (with semicircular benching to your right), pass through the squeezer stile. Immediately after this, walk along the track to the right, crossing the stream by the Matlock and District Activity Centre, before walking alongside a high wall.

At the end of the wall, take the track uphill to the left and, 50 yards before Lake Wood, take the path on the right alongside some conifers. Follow this path as it runs slowly uphill, between gardens on the left and open fields on the right. This path brings you out into Church Street, Tansley, and you can find your way back to The Tavern – down to the right if you're not sure.

20 Mapleton
The Okeover Arms

This Grade I listed building dates from about 1700. In the past it was a temperance hotel but now (fortunately for us) it is a public house. It is in a lovely, relatively quiet position next to the unusual church of St Mary, just across a field from the river Dove as it winds its way down from the hustle and bustle of Dovedale.

Good food, well priced is what the Okeover Arms aims for – and achieves. There is a wide choice, with starters, main courses and children's meals. Besides more traditional dishes, the pub has several interesting diversions – grape mayonnaise, Mayfield smoked trout, Dove trout and stuffed plaice with cheese and broccoli. A firm favourite is always cold ham, two eggs, chips, tomatoes, peas and mushrooms. Lunch is served seven days a week from noon to 2.30 pm and evening meals are available from 7 pm to 10 pm. Burton Ale and Old English are the real ale and draught cider respectively. You can enjoy these out of doors in the beer garden on fine days.

The Okeover Arms has the added bonus of a ghost. You are unlikely to see the apparition, however, as it only comes out in the early morning – unless you try the accommodation offered by the pub, of course.

Telephone: 0335 29305.

How to get there: Mapleton (or Mappleton – see some of the roadsigns thereabouts) is about 1½ miles north-west of Ashbourne, between the A52 Leek road and the A515 Buxton road. There is only one street through the village, and only one pub, so you are unlikely to miss it. Although on the whole the name of the village is spelt 'Mapleton', it is pronounced to rhyme with 'apple' (just in case you have to ask how to get there).

Parking: You may park in the pub car park, while you walk, if you ask first. The road is quiet through the village though, so it should not be difficult to find an alternative berth.

Length of the walk: 6¾ miles or 3¾ miles if you want to walk just to Coldwall Bridge and back. Maps: OS Outdoor Leisure 24 The Peak District/White Peak Area, and Pathfinder 810 Ashbourne and The Churnet Valley (GR 165479).

This walk is all about the river Dove. Basically the route takes you up one side and brings you back on the other. The Dove is the boundary between Staffordshire and Derbyshire and so the route will mean stepping out of Derbyshire for about half the walk. The river changes character as you walk away from Mapleton and some of the majesty of Dovedale is apparent as you reach the halfway stage of the walk in the dale itself. There are some steady ascents giving you lovely views.

The Walk
Standing with your back to the Okeover Arms, climb over the stile into the field, signposted 'Dovedale'. From here, walk across to the bridge in the far right-hand corner of the field. Turn left down the road for ⅓ mile, crossing Okeover bridge on the way. This road bridge is narrow, so take care. Take the footpath on the right to Coldwall Bridge and Ilam, the latter being 2½ miles away, according to the signpost. Go past the old mill and take the stile to the right of the gate. Follow the stream on the right to the far side of the field. Cross the small bridge and enter a second field. Walk through this

84

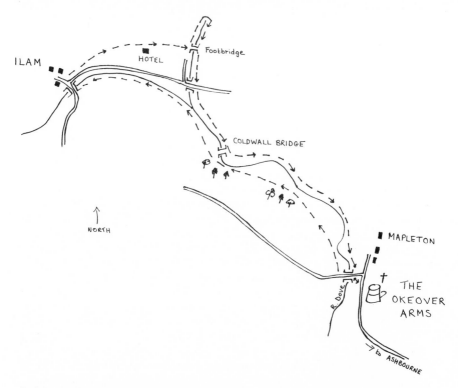

field, climbing slightly uphill as you go. Ahead you will soon see the hills around Dovedale. Climb the stile on to a farm track and turn right towards the farm (Littlepark).

Just before you get to the farm buildings – at the other side of a hedge on your left – climb over the stile. Ascend slightly to the right towards the top side of a silage dump. Once above this, turn right, walking towards the 20 ft high dead tree in the field (muddy at times) behind the farm. From the tree, walk in the general direction of the village of Thorpe – a mile or so ahead on the hillside in front of you. Climb the stile to the right of the gate at the end of the field, then walk downhill to where the wood in front joins the river. Turn left at the river and follow the path through the wood. There is usually plenty of birdlife here – look out for goldcrests, our smallest British bird.

At the end of the wood, go through the stile at the side of the gate and head through the field in front, keeping the trees on your left. You then come to another wood at the side of the river. Climb over the stile and walk through the wood. Once out of it follow the path ahead to Coldwall Bridge.

85

If you like, you can turn right over this bridge and shorten the walk by returning to Mapleton down the other side of the river, following the instructions in the last paragraph.

For the full walk, climb up the steps on to the bridge and walk a few yards to the gap in the wall opposite to follow the path to Ilam. Climb a small bank from the bridge. Over a mile away, ahead of you, is the distinctive outline of Bunster Hill. Walk through the field towards the left-hand side of the ridge in the distance. At the end of this field, go through the gate and follow the waymark over the small plank bridge – you should still be walking towards the ridge. Keep on towards the waymarked post slightly uphill from you. From here you can enjoy the view of Thorpe Cloud on the right and Bunster Hill on the left. Following the waymarks, walk on towards the river. Cross a small bridge. With the river Dove immediately to your right, walk the ½ mile or so up to Ilam. The path is quite well defined. Climb up on to the road and turn right over the road bridge.

If you want to explore Ilam and have a cup of tea (if the tearoom is open), turn left once you have crossed the bridge and walk towards the church and the hall (now a youth hostel).

The walk back to Mapleton takes you along the road to the right once you have crossed the bridge. After 150 yards, take the path through the hedge on the left and bear right, climbing slightly uphill. You will shortly join a track. From this point Ilam can be seen nestling in the valley behind you. Follow the track to the end of the field. Once into the next field walk on, heading towards the right-hand side of. Thorpe Cloud (the flat-topped hill in front). At the end of this second field, take the stile to the left of the gate and then walk towards the centre of Thorpe Cloud. Cross the next, narrow, field behind the Izaak Walton Hotel, then walk on towards the car park at the bottom of Thorpe Cloud. At the end of the field, climb the stile and follow the path down to the car park and toilets.

Turn left before the toilets and walk upriver for 100 yards on the track. You can cross the footbridge on your right at this point on to the far bank, or continue upriver for 500 yards along the track, cross over the stepping stones and then walk downriver along the far bank until you come back to the far side of the footbridge.

From the other side of the footbridge, climb the stile at the side of the bridge and take the path half-left heading down stream. Then take the (sometimes boggy) path between the river and the small plantation. At the end of the trees, bear right towards the river. The path now follows the river until you reach the road. Take care here as cars come quite quickly over St Mary's Bridge from the right.

From the bridge, turn left along the road and walk to the stile 20 yards away on the right. Cross the field from the road to a stile at the side of a gate. Keep straight on towards the stream. Cross the wooden step stile and walk on to the river. Walk down the left bank of the river back to Coldwall Bridge.

From Coldwall Bridge, turn left uphill towards the milepost (erected in 1822) marked 'Cheadle 11'. Almost immediately after turning left uphill (and before reaching the milepost), turn right down a track. After 60 yards, pass through a gate and follow the track to Dove Cottage. The path goes to the right of the cottage. Take the stile at the side of the gate and walk on through the field beyond the cottage, with the river on your right. Follow the stiles through the next few fields, walking along the river bank as you go. Approximately 1 mile beyond the cottage when you see a weir in the river to your right, cut away from the river, heading just to the right of the village in front of you. Then walk alongside the river for the next two fields, before walking slightly away from the river across the last field to the road. Cross the road to the stile into the field opposite, then walk back to the Okeover Arms.

Kniveton
The Red Lion

The Red Lion started off life as three cottages, the original village pub being at that time two doors up the road. The cottages were eventually converted into a one-room pub by Offilers Brewery and, despite being closed for three years about 20 years or so ago, it has never looked back. It is very much a village pub with locals making good use of it. Walkers are welcome though and will enjoy both the real ale and the food.

The landlord has an interesting selection of ales – Wards Sheffield Best and Burton Bridge, as well as a guest beer which changes weekly. Woodpecker and Taunton Dry Blackthorn ciders are available too. Grilled trout, sirloin steak, chilli con carne and ham, egg and chips are among the dishes on offer. What provides an interesting option is the vegetarian menu – tiropitta (fetta cheese and spring onion in filo pastry), spinach and chopped nut pastie, and chickpea curry being typical of this. In all there are about 20 main courses to choose from. Lunch is from noon until 2 pm every day and the evening meal is served from 7 pm until 9 pm.

Telephone: 0335 345554.

How to get there: Kniveton is on the B5035 about 3 miles north-east of Ashbourne. The Red Lion is in the middle of the village.

Parking: The landlord has no objection to you parking in front of the pub while you walk, but ask first. Space is somewhat limited, so you may have to find somewhere nearby in the village to leave your car.

Length of the walk: 4½ miles. Map: OS Outdoor Leisure 24 The Peak District/White Peak Area (GR 207502).

Rolling Derbyshire countryside, green fields, a few ups and downs and unusual gates (instead of stiles) make for a pleasant walk from Kniveton to Bradbourne and back.

The Walk

Walk up the road from the Red Lion, passing an old milestone showing Alfreton 16 miles and Wirksworth 6 miles away. Just beyond the Norman church of St Michael, turn left along the road in front of the village hall. About 350 yards later, after passing The Hallsteads, you arrive at The Closes caravan park. The road bears round to the left at this point. You should leave it here and walk along the tarmac lane in front, ignoring first a track to the right alongside a garden, then a track to the left after 300 yards. The lane you are on takes you to, and then past, Newhouse Farm. Around 400 yards after the farm, the lane swings right. You should leave it here and take the rougher track ahead alongside the fence. Follow this as it descends to Havenhill Dale Brook, roughly ½ mile ahead. As you get nearer the valley bottom the imposing slope on your left is Haven Hill. Cross the brook to the road.

Follow the road to the left, passing Bank House and Ivy Cottage to a T-junction. Turn left into the village, past Bradbourne Hall on the right. At the lamp (which commemorates the Diamond Jubilee of Queen Victoria) you can turn right to the church. The key to gain entry is available on request. Just inside the entrance to the churchyard is an ancient 8th century Celtic cross.

To continue the walk, keep on the road past the lamp on your right. Just beyond the playground at the end of the village, pass through the stile on your left. Walk half-right to the stile across the field, then veer slightly left to the next stile, in the hedge. From here go half-right in the direction of the building on the distant hillside. You are now walking in a line vaguely parallel to the Havenhill Dale Brook below to your left. This path leads you to a farm gate. Pass through this and then the stile, 10 yards beyond in the thorn trees.

When you have got through the thorns, turn left downhill to the footbridge. Cross over this and the smaller one beyond. The buildings

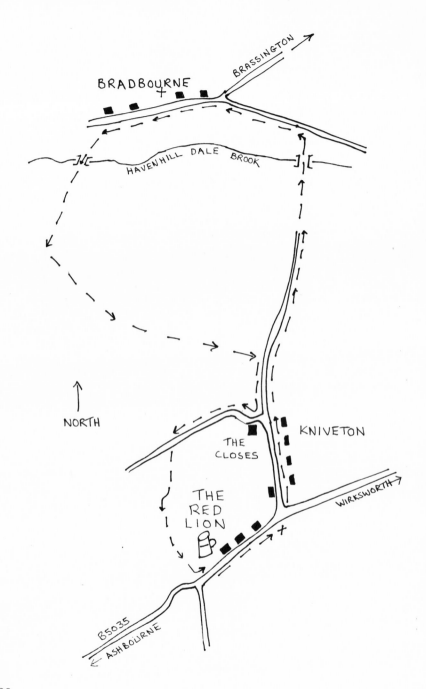

BRADBOURNE

BRASSINGTON

HAVENHILL DALE BROOK

NORTH

KNIVETON

THE CLOSES

THE RED LION

WIRKSWORTH

B5035

ASHBOURNE

90

downstream are Bradbourne Mill. After crossing the smaller bridge, turn right alongside the brook to the stile in the hedge 30 yards away.

Once you are over the stile and through the hedge, walk straight ahead (uphill) through the thorn trees on the hillside ahead of you. Bear slightly left as the field becomes more open. You are now nearer the farm you saw from across the other side of the valley. You should walk towards a gate one field to the left of this farm – a gate with a line of trees running away from it. After passing through it, walk along the green lane alongside the trees, with the farm across the other side of a field to your right.

At the end of this track, pass through the small gate. Walk on the left-hand side of the field to the small walled section of track for 25 or 30 yards to a gate. Keep on the right side of the next field with Wigber Low on your left. A low in these parts is a high piece of ground. Not so far away there is a village called Highlow. Stay on the right-hand side of the next field for about 180 yards. After passing through the gate (where the wall changes angle slightly to the left), walk forward along the left side of the broken line of trees in front, before bearing left towards the farm to your left. As you get near to this farm go through the gate into a short stretch of green lane. Then continue forward, with the outbuildings and stables on your left. The only building on your right is a small red-brick one. At the end of the buildings, walk on along the track. After passing a red-brick house on the left, you come back to the lane you walked along earlier. Turn right, back to The Closes.

From here you can either retrace your route to the pub, or turn right to walk back a different way. If you turn right watch out for some narrow kissing-gates.

For the new route, walk for 350 yards or so to the right past The Closes. Look out on your left for one of the kissing-gates that are just about unique to Kniveton. This is just in front of a track cutting into the fields on your left between two hedges. Pass through the kissing-gate on your left, to leave the road. Walk down the right-hand side of the first two fields after the road. Halfway through the third field, turn right through a stile at the side of a farm gate. Then turn left and follow the path, heading towards a sunken lane about 70 yards later. Pass through another kissing-gate. This leads you to a track which then takes you into the village and back to the Red Lion.

Shirley
The Saracen's Head

Shirley's claim to fame is that Bonnie Prince Charlie is said to have spent the night in the village in 1745, during his abortive attempt to seize the English throne.

The Saracen's Head is popular with locals as well as walkers and others passing through and you can be sure of a good welcome. It is the only pub in this pretty village and supplies good, tasty meals to those in need. For example, home-made steak and mushroom pie is on offer, as well as scampi, plaice dieppoise (stuffed with prawns and mushrooms), chicken Kiev, and lasagne (verde or vegetable), amongst others. Sweets include spotted dick with custard and sticky toffee pudding with custard. There is also a children's menu which includes sausage, or chicken burger in a bun with chips and baked beans. Snacks are also available, including filled rolls, jacket potatoes, toasties and pizza with extra toppings. Lunch is served from noon to 2 pm every day and evening meals from 7 pm to 8.45 pm on Monday to Saturday evenings. There are also occasional specials, such as fresh trout and a wonderful rabbit pie. A choice of real ales is usually available – Hoskins and Oldfield HOB Bitter, Marston's Pedigree, Draught Bass and Courage Directors being on offer at different times,

plus Strongbow draught cider. A beer garden at the front of the pub is a great draw when the weather is good.
Telephone: 0335 60330.

How to get there: Shirley lies just under 4 miles south-east of Ashbourne, off the A52, which runs between Ashbourne and Derby. The Saracen's Head is near St Michael's church.

Parking: There is a small car park at the pub. This can be used, while you walk, if you ask first. Parking is also possible on the road nearby.

Length of the walk: 4¾ miles. Maps: OS Pathfinder 810 Ashbourne and The Churnet Valley and 811 Belper (GR 218416).

Two pretty villages of quite different character are linked by this relatively flat route. If you have the opportunity, walk it when the daffodils are out − you will be in for a floral treat as you go out of Shirley along Park Lane. It really is a lovely area at any time of year, though.

The Walk

Turn left from the pub, walking slightly uphill on the road. Pass the church on your right and the Old School House. When the road turns sharply right at the edge of the village, carry straight on down Park Lane, where there are thousands of daffodils in the springtime.

Keep on the lane past Shirley House on the left and the playing fields on the right. As you come to the edge of the wood, pass through the gate but keep on the track. Walk past Shirley Park Farm on your right. Soon after the farm, pass through the gap at the side of the gate. Keep to the track, with the fields on your right and woodland on your left. About 400 yards beyond the gate, the track levels out and you come to a junction of paths and tracks. Your route follows the track straight ahead which descends quite steeply through the woodland. Soon after you start to descend, you will see the lake in the valley bottom. There are usually quite a few wildfowl on the water. Before you reach the waterside, however, look out for Osmaston Sawmill on the left, a lovely building set in the woodland.

Follow the track ahead, with the lake on your right. Then climb uphill with fields on either side. Keep on this track (which is, in fact, a bridleway) until you come to the edge of Osmaston village, ignoring a fork to the right at the top of the hill before the bridleway levels out and leads into the village, which is full of thatched cottages. The village pond is in front of you. Go and look closely at the seat to its left.

Having walked into the village on the bridleway and looking towards the pond, turn left through the rather ornate gateway. Pass

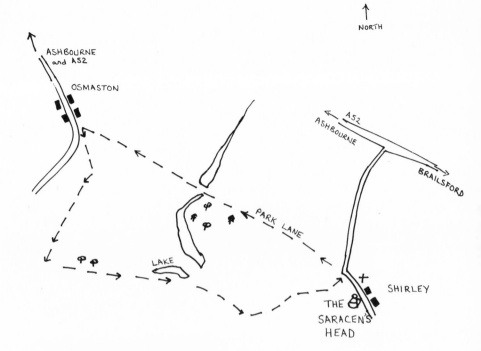

NORTH

The Lodge and continue along the driveway before taking the first
turn right. Stay on this track, taking no notice of the right turn into
the playing fields. Walk past the black and white timber house on the
left – sometimes hidden by heavy foliage. At the T-junction turn
right, at which point the bridleway comes out into the open. Pass
another house on your right. Follow this track for about ½ mile,
ignoring any tracks to the right. In the valley, pass through the gate
and then at the end of the trees, pass through another gate. Turn left
at quite an acute angle, once you are through this gate. Walk along
through the fields, with the trees on your left. There are squeezer stiles
ahead of you. Climb over the first three of these stiles before arriving
at the side of another (smallish) lake.

At the end of the lake, keep ahead through the stile at the side of
a gate, ignoring the left turn. Follow the track through the wood. Stay
on the level, disregarding the track uphill to the right and the track a
little further on to the left. Continue, passing through conifers. Once
you reach the edge of the wood, walk through the gateway and turn
left. Follow the path round the edge of the marshy ground to the
footbridge 200 or so yards away. Sometimes a 10 yard section of the
path in this wet area can be 'bouncy', actually moving under you as

94

you walk over it. Cross the footbridge over the brook and proceed to the small gate in front of you, climbing over the stile at the side, then walk up the right-hand side of the field. Approximately 30 yards from the end of the field, climb the stile on your right, walking half-right diagonally across the field towards the gate. You should be walking in the general direction of the house on the hill in front of you. Climb through the stile at the side of the gate and proceed up the left-hand side of the field. Just after the gateway, climb the stile into the field on your left. Keep round the right-hand side of the field and head for the house on the hill.

There appears to be some doubt where the public footpath actually goes at this point. Some say on the left side of the hedge, some say on the other side, between the house and the hedge. A map supplied by the local District Council shows it on the left side. As most walkers seem to stay in the field, you may feel you will do the same, so keep left of the hedge. When you get near the top of the field, pass through a stile on your right and turn left towards the lane. Walk down some steps and you are back into Park Lane. Turn right, back into the village and continue to the Saracen's Head.

㉓ Mugginton
The Cock Inn

The Cock is well sited if you fancy a day out in the rolling countryside just to the north-west of Derby. Start with this 5 mile walk, then recharge your batteries with a drink and lunch at the pub. You can then decide whether to spend the afternoon having a stroll round Carsington Water (4 miles north of the Cock) or looking round Kedleston Hall, a National Trust property, on the way back to Derby.

The Cock is a 16th century coaching inn. The present restaurant used to be the stables. Marston's Pedigree is always available, as well

as draught Guinness, McEwans lager and draught mild. There is a regular guest beer, for example, Abbot Ale. Strongbow and Woodpecker draught ciders are also sold. The meals are served from noon to 2 pm and from 7 pm to 9.30 pm every day. The Cock tries to present a traditional menu and is known for its steak. A number of interesting specials are also offered, such as tournedos Rossini, pork oriental, devilled kidneys, beef Wellington, Somerset gammon and game pie, all appearing on the blackboard at different times.
Telephone: 0773 550293.

How to get there: The Cock Inn is to the north-west of Derby, lying between the A517 and the A52. Once you have found Weston Underwood on your road map, take the road heading north from there towards Muggintonlane End, about 1½ miles north. Just over ¾ mile to the north of Weston Underwood you will see the inn on your left.

Parking: There is plenty of space in the inn car park but ask first, if you want to leave your car while you walk.

Length of the walk: 5 miles. Map: OS Pathfinder 811 Belper (GR 287440).

This is an interesting route, a little off the beaten track, but well worth the effort of finding its starting point. The amount of wildlife hereabouts is surprising. On just one occasion, I saw heron, snipe, sparrowhawk, rabbits and a weasel. Unexpectedly, towards the end of the walk, there is a poignant reminder of the men and women who lost their lives during the Second World War. The walking is fairly easy and it will be an enjoyable half day's ramble.

The Walk
From the main road, walk about 10 yards down Church Lane, behind the Cock Inn. Turn right at the signpost and walk down the track towards the white house in the wood in front. Bear right, round to the front of the house. Keep just to the left of the buildings along the grassy path ahead. This descends through a mix of garden and woodland. It narrows as it goes downhill into the thicker woodland. You then come to a small gate in a fence. After going through this, bear slightly right in the direction of the pole on the hillside to your right. Go through the largish gap in the hedgerow before walking along the right-hand side of the hedge. This leads to the buildings of Old Covert Farm. Pass through the gate on to the track.

Take the stile at the side of the gate opposite and walk forward, with the farm on your left. This takes you up the right-hand side of a broken

97

line of trees. Climb the hill to a stile at the side of a gate. Negotiate this and walk forward to join a track leading to the farm ahead, dated 1728. After passing through the gate, turn left along the track alongside the red-brick building and, 10 yards or so later, turn right at the end of this. Turn almost immediately left, with the haybarn to your right. Walk out of the farmyard via the gate at the end of the farm buildings.

Follow the (sometimes muddy) track towards the gate in front. As you get nearer the end of the field you will see there are, in fact, two gates. Cross the stile to the left of the right-hand gate. Stay on this track (with a steep bank in the field over the hedge to your left), passing through another gate. Climb the stile at the side of the next gate. From this point the path carries on along the left-hand side of a hawthorn hedge. This is quite a long field, with a small wood at the far end to the left. When you come to the end of the field, climb the stile to the left of the gate and cross to the gate opposite. After you have gone through it, keep along the left side of the hedge in front and, 50 or 60 yards before the end of the field, bear left uphill towards the top corner. This brings you to a squeezer stile and on to a track. Turn left on this track and pass through a gate at the end of it. Stay on the left side of the field to another gate. This is lovely English countryside – green fields, rolling hills and hedgerows – totally unspoilt, except for the pylons on the horizon.

Climb the stile next to the gate. Turn right along the bridleway, down the hedgeside towards the bridlegate at the bottom. To your left is Mugginton church and to your right is marshy ground. The air around you is usually full of birdsong. Turn left at an acute angle before the bridlegate and walk along the left-hand side of the hedge. This takes you in the general direction of Mugginton itself. The path appears to be an old sunken lane and eventually leads you to a farmgate. Cross the stile at the side and follow the track. Stay on this as it brings you into the village, passing a pair of interesting ponds as well as Calder Farm and other attractive buildings on the way. The track becomes a tarmac lane known as Taghole Lane, before climbing uphill into the village.

Turn right down Church Lane if you want to visit the church. With an ancient yew tree and box pews, it is worth seeing and usually open.

From the end of Taghole Lane take the farm track between the telephone box and the letterbox. Continue straight on, staying to the left of the long, open cowshed. Beyond this, follow the track to a view of Weston Underwood across the fields in front of you. Walk along the track as it crosses the first field to a gateway. Do not pass through the gateway but walk down the right-hand side of the hedge to the bottom of the field and Greenlane Brook. Cross the footbridge. Walk diagonally right but keep to the left of the big tree in the middle of the

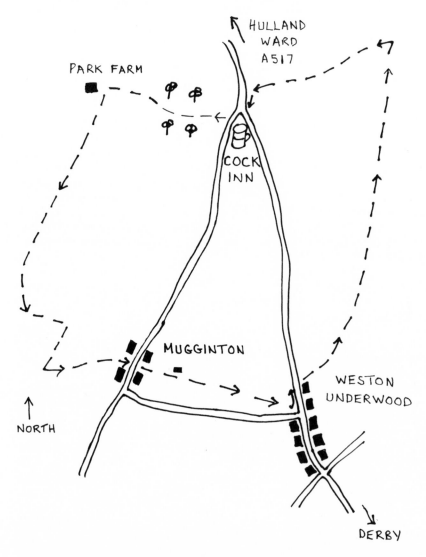

HULLAND
WARD
A517

PARK FARM

COCK
INN

MUGGINTON

WESTON
UNDERWOOD

NORTH

DERBY

field. As you climb slightly uphill you will see in the far corner of the field a gate and signpost. Walk towards these.

Turn left on Green Lane then left again on the main road and walk into the village of Weston Underwood. Immediately past Mauna Kea on the right-hand side of the road, turn right at the signpost and walk between the fences, then the hedges, to a gate into a field. Stay on the left side of the fence until you come to a stile. Climb this. Walk parallel to the field boundary on your left to reach the stile approximately 70 yards to the right of the far left corner of the field. This stile leads you into a rough grassy area. Follow the winding path, keeping as near to the fence on your right as possible. Go straight forward, between the hedge and the old quarry. The quarry has not been used for some time and Mother Nature is slowly taking control to create a wonderful haven for local flora and fauna.

At the end of the disused pit, walk into the open field for 20 yards, then go through the gateway on your right. Walk along the left side of the next field towards the largish dead tree at the far end. This path runs along a line parallel to the hedge, 30 yards or so into the field. Most people seem to walk along the hedge though. Cross the stile at the old tree. Walk towards the stile opposite and keep straight on beyond this to the stile at the far side, 150 yards or so away. As you cross the next field to the stile, you will see to the right a memorial to airmen who died in this field when their Armstrong Whitley bomber crashed during the Second World War. All five airmen, aged between 18 and 24 years, were killed. There is no footpath directly to the memorial and so, strictly speaking, you will have to view this from afar. Please remember that this is private land and you should stay on the public footpaths. On Remembrance Day each year a service is held here, and afterwards everyone usually adjourns to the Cock Inn.

Once you have crossed this largish field, keep ahead in the next field towards the hedge jutting out into the field between you and the masts on the horizon. These are on Alport Heights, a National Trust property with marvellous views of the surrounding countryside. Walk on with the hedge on your left to the gateway in the corner of the field ahead of you. Pass through this gate and, with the hedge still on your left, proceed for 20 or 30 yards into the next field. Go through the gate into the field to your left and turn right to walk alongside the hedge. The path descends gradually to a track. Turn left along this for some distance and follow it back to the Cock Inn.

Farnah Green
The Bluebell Inn and Restaurant

Although the Bluebell is a little off the beaten track, it is well worth seeking out. Located at Farnah Green about a mile to the west of Belper, this 18th century up-market pub is pleasing to the eye both inside and outside.

The food can be thoroughly recommended and you can look forward to an interesting and enjoyable meal. Bacon and black pudding brunch, Sloppy Joe, Farnahburger, Bluebell farmhouse grill and Bluebell smokies can all be sampled during the day. In the evening the meals are just as good. Examples are sauté of beef with mushroom and green pepper sauce, and pan-fried venison liver with grilled bacon and onion – both delicious. Real ale in the form of Bass Bitter can be sampled either inside or in the beer garden. Meals are served from noon until 2 pm every day except Monday and from 7 pm to 9.30 pm Tuesday to Saturday (inclusive). Because the Bluebell is so popular, the weekends are very busy and it may be advisable to book a table if you want to eat there on a Saturday or Sunday.

Telephone: 0773 826495.

101

How to get there: The inn is in Farnah Green, to the south of the A517 Ashbourne to Belper road. Turn off at the Hazelwood sign, less than a mile from Belper itself. The Bluebell is approximately ¾ mile away on your right.

Parking: Use the Bluebell's car park (with permission), while you walk, or park along the road just on the north side of the inn. Alternatively you can park in a layby at Firestone Hill, 600 yards or so south of the Bluebell, and walk back to the inn.

Length of the walk: 5¼ miles. Map: OS Pathfinder 811 Belper (GR 335468).

Another walk outside the Peak District but none the worse for that – some of the views on this walk are excellent. There are a couple of climbs, one of them at the end of the walk. This is an area well worth exploring. For bird-watchers in particular Wyver Lane Pool further along is worth walking to.

The Walk
With the Bluebell Inn behind you, turn left on the road and, 200 yards later, turn left down the first drive to Fearn House (not the second drive the far side of the fence). Keep to the right all the way down the track. Pass through the stile at the side of the gate. Straight opposite, pass through the next stile. Walk along the right-hand side of the field. In the far corner, climb over the stone step stile – do not take the kissing-gate, no more than a yard away on the left, as this is private.

Once over the stone step stile, turn right along the level path between the fern or bracken and into the woodland. Climb over a fence/stile before walking towards a stile at the far end. Climb out of the wood to a view of lovely rolling countryside in front. Walk slightly downhill through the field, keeping parallel to the hedge on the left, towards the large tree. Climb over the stile and walk forward for 15 or 20 yards to another stile opposite.

Climb out on to the rough track. Turn right and follow it for the next 500 yards, walking through (or over) a ford just before reaching the road. Turn right on the road. Pass Plains Lane on the left. Turn left shortly afterwards, up Long Walls Lane. This is an ancient route, used at least as far back as Saxon times. It may even be an old Roman road. As you walk up the lane, turn round and look back to the line of trees on the hillside behind you. These lie on the original route of this old road. One of the great joys of walking is the chance to discover the past. Travellers have used this lane for hundreds of years, possibly for as many as 2,000.

Pass Holly House and then the entrance to Handley Grange. The

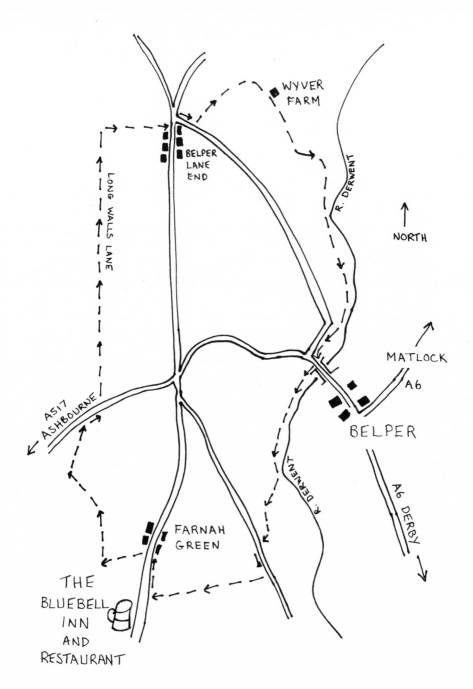

WYVER FARM

BELPER LANE END

LONG WALLS LANE

R. DERWENT

NORTH

MATLOCK
A6

A517
ASHBOURNE

BELPER

R. DERWENT

A6 DERBY

FARNAH GREEN

THE
BLUEBELL
INN
AND
RESTAURANT

tarmac lane becomes a sandy track with trees either side. The track levels out and a number of paths cross the lane. Ignore them all until you come to a wood a field away on your right. This wood runs parallel to the track. About 200 yards beyond the start of the wood, turn right across the field into the trees. Pass through the wood (only 50 yards or so) and into a field on the other side. Walk down the left side of the field, along the wallside, toward the buildings in front. Pass through the stile and down the track to the road at Belper Lane End.

Turn left along the lane towards the Bull's Head, where three lanes come together. Turn right, down the road signed 'Belper Lane End'. At Chapel House, turn left along the bridleway. Pass through the gate and into the field beyond. In this and the next field, stay on the left. In the second field pass through a gate to lead along the third field towards Wyver Farm ahead. At the end of the grassy track, go through the gate into the farmyard.

Walk through Wyver Farm, along the track as it slowly descends in front of you. Take no notice of the track rising to the right. Stay to the left of the red-brick building at the end of the farmyard. As you continue along the track, the river Derwent and Wyver Lane Pool are in view to your left. The latter is a Derbyshire Wildlife Trust nature reserve and is usually full of wildfowl.

Pass through a gate and the track takes you along the right-hand side of a field and then bears left towards the river. Go through the gate marked 'Wyver Farm' on the far side, and turn right on the tarmac track at the side of the pond. Pass the Derbyshire Wildlife Trust sign. Ignoring the footpath to the right just beyond the pool, stay on the tarmac lane parallel to the river. This eventually leads to some houses. Across the river on your left is the red-brick East Mill (1912) and also the River Gardens. When you come to the road at Bridge Foot, turn left. Ignore the road to the right up Bridge Hill beside the Talbot Hotel and keep straight on, as though you were going to cross the Derwent. Before you do so, turn right down the tarmac path, with the green metal railings on your left. Looking back across the river, you have another view of East Mill and the road bridge.

Stay on the path until you come to a small brick building and pass through the stile to its right. Walk along this path, on the right-hand side of a wall, slowly moving away from the river. Pass through another stile and then cross a small bridge over a brook. Take the stile on the left of the gate on the bridge. Walk forward alongside the fence, then straight forward through the field in front, keeping to the left of the stone stoop in the middle of the field. Approximately 70 yards beyond this stoop, you come to the corner of a wall jutting out into the field on the right. Walk past this, and you will find you are walking near to the river again. Look out for the second gate on the right, about halfway through the field. Pass through the stile to the left of this gate. Bear diagonally left, climbing gently in the direction of the house on the hill in front. Stay on this line, before bearing further left in the field below the house. This brings you to the end of a wall with a hedge above. At the corner, turn right to walk between the barbed wire fence and the hedge. Walk forward down the driveway onto the road, passing through the gate marked 'The Swiss House'.

Turn left on the road. Just over 100 yards later, in the field before the bungalow, turn right at the signpost. Walk straight up the right-hand side of the two fields in front to come out onto a sandy track. The view of Belper from here is well worth studying, with the East Mill quite prominent. Follow Sandy Lane to the right for 10 yards before turning left out onto the road. The Bluebell Inn is visible to the left from here.

㉕ Whatstandwell
The Derwent Hotel

The hotel is on the A6, next to the bridge over the Derwent. It is nearly 300 years old and part of it was originally a toll house. It has also been used as a coaching inn and the original blacksmith's forge is still in existence next door. Tradition has it that one Walter Standwell used to be tollmaster here in the 1700s, hence the name Whatstandwell. Another story has it that a Walter Stonewell lived hereabouts centuries ago. Anyone interested in fishing as well as walking and eating will find the Derwent Hotel to their liking. It owns the fishing rights for ¼ mile along the river Derwent and day tickets are available (they are free if you are staying at the hotel). Anyone wanting a good day in the countryside could start with a walk in the morning, then have lunch at the Derwent and finish off fishing *in* the Derwent. The hotel would also be a good centre from which to visit the surrounding area and try out some of the other walks in the book.

The meals are good value and everything from a sandwich to a steak is served. The comprehensive menu includes mixed grill, moussaka, lasagne, home-made steak and ale pie, home-made cheese and onion pie, chicken in tarragon, as well as vegetarian dishes such as wheat and walnut casserole and cauliflower and chickpea korma curry. Meals are

served at lunchtime each day from noon to 2.30 pm. In the evening food is available from 6 pm to 9 pm Monday to Thursday; 6 pm to 9.30 pm Friday and Saturday and 7 pm to 9 pm Sunday. This is a Kimberley pub serving Kimberley Best, Classic and Best Mild. Strongbow and Woodpecker draught ciders are also on offer. Children are welcome and there is a family room and a beer garden, and even a patio with an aviary and pets corner.
Telephone: 0773 856616.

How to get there: You will find the hotel at the junction of the B5035 with the A6, partway between Matlock and Belper.

Parking: The landlord is happy to let you park at the hotel, while you walk, but requests you to ask him first. There is also some parking up the hill from the hotel (Main Road) – turn sharp left to park alongside the canal.

Length of the walk: 5 miles. Map: OS Outdoor Leisure 24 The Peak District/White Peak Area (GR 332544).

Distant views, canalside walking, woodlands, and the chance to visit Crich, the village involved in the filming of 'Peak Practice', combine to make this a really enjoyable walk. There is a steady climb from the canal to Crich Stand and steps inside the Stand to the top. On a clear day the view from here is excellent, so take some binoculars with you.

The Walk
From the Derwent Hotel walk up Main Road. After ascending for approximately 100 yards, turn left along the canal. About 400 yards later there is a footbridge over the canal. Just 50 yards before it, take the path to the left which leads you up to the bridge and over the canal. The path then forks left and heads away from the canal through the wood, to the road. Cross the road and follow the track heading into the trees, ignoring the path 12 or 15 yards from the road to the right. Also ignore other paths to the right leading into the quarries on that side of the path. After crossing a bridge over a stream towards the end of the wood, ignore the stile to the left into the field. Carry straight on for a further 50 yards, climbing over the stile out of the wood and into the field. Straight ahead on the horizon, Crich Stand, a stone memorial tower and beacon, can be seen through the trees. Beyond this field, walk through the small wood. The path continues up the centre of the field, curving to the left to the stile onto the road.
Turn right at the road, then, 20 yards later, turn left up the track at 'Staddlestone'. Stay on this track, walking towards Cliff Farm directly

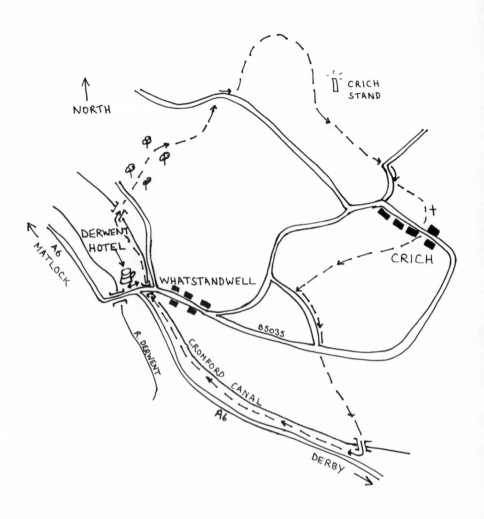

in front of you. Take the path leading up to the right, 50 yards before the farmhouse. Follow this path as it ascends – you may see the trams from the Tramway Museum above you to the right. Bear right and cross the tramline. Proceed up the rough track, following the line of electricity poles. Where it levels out, bear right slightly uphill, ignoring the path over the stile to the left. Stay with the track, which leads you towards the Stand, a memorial to the Sherwood Foresters. There is a box for donations just inside the entrance to the tower. It is usually open so do climb it. Before you do so, you may wish to visit the shop and café 100 yards away down the hill, where a leaflet is available pointing out what can be seen from the top of the tower. Lincoln

Cathedral is apparently visible on a clear day, 41 miles away. So is Belvoir Castle, just 32 miles from the Stand.

Once you have looked around, walk away from the tower towards Crich church. On the right as you descend the tarmac drive is the shop and café. Once you have left the driveway leading to Crich Stand, keep on along the road ahead towards the church. Bear right, round the corner. Just before the stone building on the left, pass through the stile at the side of the gate. Walk in the general direction of the church. Stay on the right-hand side of the first and second fields, then slightly left in the third. Pass through the kissing-gate beside the old barn, into the churchyard. Turn right and walk round to the front of the church.

From the church porch, go to the gate and cross the road. Walk between Horseshoe Cottage and the house with 'No 9' on it, to the stiles beside the two gates. Then walk in a direct line down the right-hand side of the field. Before the stone bridge on your right, climb the stile to walk over the bridge itself. Carry straight on in the next field. Just over halfway along the wallside, pass through the stile at the gateway, then go immediately left up the wallside. Head slightly away from the wall towards the gap stile ahead between the two gateways.

Proceed towards the next stile in front and walk down the right-hand side of the next field, with a wide view of the surrounding area in front. The masts on the horizon are Alport Heights, and the white building just below is Alderwasley Hall. Walk down the left of the following field. Keep straight on in the next field, but stay just to the right of the buildings of Benthill Farm. Quickly descend along the path, then down the steps, to the road below.

Turn left along the road before descending Shaws Hill to a busier road. The views from this hillside across the Derwent valley are splendid. At the bottom of Shaws Hill, a strategically placed seat overlooking the valley gives you an excellent opportunity to survey the wonderful panorama.

When you are ready, walk down the track to the left of the seat. Stay on this track, ignoring the 'Private' sign, and descend through the trees to the Cromford Canal. Cross the bridge over the canal before turning right on the far side of the bridge and walking down to it. Walk along the towpath, with the canal on your right, for approximately 1 mile. This stretch of the canal runs parallel to the railway line, the A6 and the river Derwent. Pass under the footbridge near Whatstandwell railway station. Then at the stone road bridge shortly afterwards, turn left down the road and return to the Derwent Hotel.

Positioned on the busy A6 about halfway between Ambergate and Matlock the Homesford Cottage is well frequented. Walkers are welcome and good food will sustain them.

Meals are served every lunchtime from noon until 2.30 pm and from 7 pm to 9.45 pm Monday to Friday or 7 pm to 10 pm Saturday and Sunday. The food is reasonably priced and includes a wide range, from snacks (including steak sandwich and bacon butty) to starters (soup, cheese dip) to main dishes (scampi, vegetable lasagne, mixed grill, steak, salads) to sweets (spotted dick and gâteaux). Kimberley Best Bitter and Best Mild are both for sale, plus Strongbow draught cider. The pub has a no-smoking area as well as a beer garden and an outside area specifically for children.

Telephone: 0629 822342.

How to get there: The Homesford Cottage is about 3½ miles south of Matlock on the A6. 'Homesford Cottage' is writ large on a rooftop on your left, if you are travelling down from Matlock, so look out for this. The car park is just beyond, on the other side of the road from the pub.

Parking: Let the landlady know you are parking in the car park, while you walk, even if it is only a note under the windscreen.

Length of the walk: 2½ miles. Map: OS Outdoor Leisure 24 The Peak District/White Peak Area (GR 324554).

The walk takes you past the former home of Florence Nightingale and then along the Cromford Canal. This is a lovely wooded area and there is plenty of wildlife to be seen. The canal is, in fact, a nature reserve.

The Walk

From Homesford Cottage, walk along the A6 to the right towards Belper past the car park on your left. Take the first turn left beyond the car park, and follow the tarmac drive under the railway tunnel. Then take the path to the right, which leads to a footbridge over the river Derwent. Cross this and follow the path to the left through the wood. Where the path divides, take the right fork and turn right after the stile. You are now above the canal tunnel. Walk uphill for a few

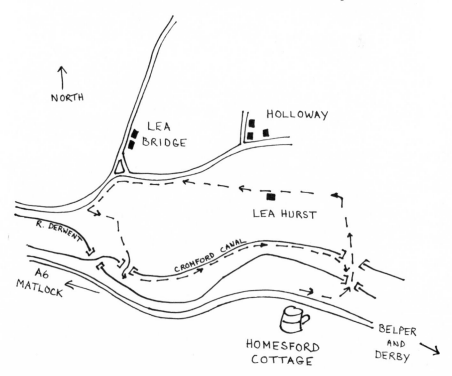

yards and pass through the kissing-gate on the left into the field. Walk up the field beside the high deer fence. Keep to the left of the house partway up the field, then keep on the track towards the kissing-gate at the top.

As you climb this field, you can see to the left Lea Hurst and to your right Crich Stand (which is visited in Walk 25). Lea Hurst was originally the home of Florence Nightingale, and it is now a residential home. Once you have gone through the kissing-gate at the top of the field, turn left and walk alongside the hedge towards Lea Hurst. Go through the stiles at either side of the private drive leading to it. Carry on alongside the fence on the far side of the drive, towards the stile 30 yards further on. Once through this stile, bear left along the stone wall. Where the wall straightens out, head slightly right to the stile in front of the small copse just downhill of you. Walk through the copse and then, once out of it, follow the wallside on your right as the path slowly descends.

Climb the stile in the fence and keep forward again until the path bears to the right on to the road. Turn left down the road, ignoring both roads turning off to the right. Keep down the hill, bearing left at the bottom round the corner, and cross the stream in the process. Walk down the road for 200 yards towards the small cluster of houses. Before the right-hand bend, look out for a footpath signpost on the right-hand side of the road. Go down the driveway on the left, opposite the sign, between Lea Wood Cottage and Lea Wood House. After crossing the stream only a few yards later, turn left, then follow the path round beside a high wall on your right.

At the end of the wall, turn right towards the house. Keep to the left of this. Walk alongside the stream, crossing the Derby–Matlock railway line at Leawood Tunnel. Once you reach the Cromford Canal, cross the bridge and turn left alongside it. Look out for pike floating motionless in the water. You may even be fortunate enough to see kingfishers.

Stay by the canal for ⅔ mile, until you see the canal tunnel. Just 20 or 30 yards before the tunnel, take the path to the right through the wood. You are then back on the route you walked from the pub. So, cross the footbridge, walk under the railway tunnel and follow the drive back up to the A6 and Homesford Cottage.

Dalbury Lees
The Black Cow

The Black Cow featured in this walk stands near the green in the small village of Lees in the parish of Dalbury Lees, Dalbury being a hamlet 2 miles south of Lees. It was built around 1790 and has always been a pub or an alehouse. Surrounded by pasture land for cattle, the pub supplies good, simple food and is popular with locals as well as others from further afield.

The meals are good value and you can expect to choose from steak, gammon, scampi, chicken, cheese and tomato pizza, toasted sandwiches, chicken and mushroom pie, steak pie and sausage, and egg and chips. Lunchtime meals are served from noon to 1.30 pm every day and from 6 pm to 8.30 pm every evening, except Sunday. There are three real ales to sample – Ind Coope Burton Ale, Ansells Best Bitter and Marston's Pedigree. For the cider drinkers, Gaymers Olde English is available. There is a good-sized beer garden with swings and a see-saw for the children.

Telephone: 0332 824297.

How to get there: The Black Cow is approximately 5 miles west of the centre of Derby, and lies between the A52 Ashbourne road and the

A516 Uttoxeter road. Turn off the A52 in Kirk Langley. Just ½ mile later, turn right into Long Lane, an old Roman road. After 1½ miles, turn left towards the village of Lees.

Parking: You can park in and around the village green, while you walk, or in the pub car park, with the permission of the landlord.

Length of the walk: 3½ miles. Map: OS Pathfinder 832 Derby and Etwall (GR 265372).

This is probably the flattest walk in the book. It is an easy one and relatively unfrequented. Trusley is an attractive hamlet and worth exploring.

The Walk
With your back to the Black Cow, turn left and walk down the lane, with the village green on your right. After passing the last house on your right, take the stile just beyond the end of the garden. Walk straight ahead, parallel to the hedge about 35 yards away on your right, towards the mounds over 100 yards in front of you. Pass between the mounds and the hedge and look for the stile on your right. Cross this and turn left down to the stile in the fence to the left of the farm. Once you have crossed this, keep on towards the far right-hand corner of the field – the stile is 20 yards to the left of the corner. In the next field, head towards the far right-hand corner again. This brings you out into a green lane. Turn left along it.

About 100 yards later (at the end of the field on your left), turn right across a double plank bridge over a ditch and through the hedge. Turn left alongside the hedge. Keep on to pass the buildings of Woodhouse Farm on your left. Ahead is a stile at the side of a gate. Go over the tarmac drive to this, cross it and then cross the stile at the other side of the triangular paddock.

This brings you into a large field. Keeping to the right of the remains of a small pond, now full of trees, walk forward. You will come to a broken line of four or five trees across the field. Walk to the gate to the right of these trees and pass over the stile there. Cross the road to the stile opposite. Walk down the right-hand side of the first field, crossing to the right over the stile in the wire fence about 30 yards before the end of the field. Then turn left and walk along the left-hand side of the field to another stile. After crossing this, you will find yourself in a long, narrow field. Head down towards the end of it, bearing left, slightly before the end, to climb the fence at the bottom. From here walk forward to the footbridge 100 yards away. After you have crossed the bridge, walk up the left side of the next two fields. Just 30 yards before the end of the second field, keep straight on,

114

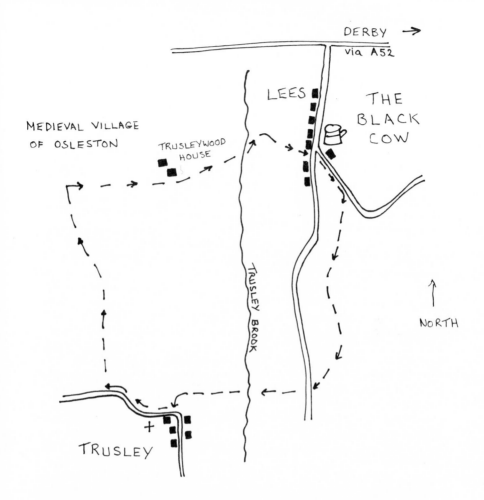

aiming for the stile. This is 40 yards to the right of the gate exiting on to a narrow tarmac lane.

Turn left along this lane (Taylor's Lane) before turning right at the T-junction. You are now in Trusley, a collection of attractive brick houses. Walk up the lane. Just before the farm on the right (where the road bends right), pass through the small wooden gate to the left to have a closer look at the 18th century church. This is not usually open, which is a pity. It is built of bricks and has an interesting door and archway. Returning to the lane, continue along it, passing Ivy Close Farm.

After the lane has proceeded round a right-hand and then a left-hand bend, pass through the second gate on your right. This is no more than 70 yards from the bend behind you. Walk straight ahead from the gate for about 170 yards, keeping just to the left of the hedge jutting out from the right. Cross the stile in the hedge, about 10 yards beyond the point where the hedge juts out. Once over the hedge, turn left and walk down the left-hand side of a long field. In the corner, cross the stile and stay on the left side of the next field. In the top left corner of this field, pass through the gate facing you, then walk diagonally left across the field to the far corner. Cross the stile in this corner and then the stile 10 yards away in front of you. The path then heads up the right-hand side of this field for 50 yards or so. Cross the stile 10 yards to the left of the corner of the field. Then walk nearly 200 yards straight ahead – even when the hedge on your right turns right at a 90 degree angle. Pass through the stile in front and walk towards another stile straight ahead, but do not pass through this one. From the stile, you can see ahead (to your left) a broken line of trees – beyond this is all that remains of the medieval village of Osleston.

Turn right, in front of the stile, to walk down to the bottom left-hand corner. Ahead of you can be seen Trusleywood House Farm. Go over the single plank bridge and the stile. Bear slightly left to the stile at the gate. From here head slightly right to the stile 20 yards away, then walk towards the gate just to the right of the farm. Cross the stile. Pass in front of the farm towards the drive. Once over this, cross the stile then walk to the far left corner of the field. Climb through into the next field. Walk half-right towards the stream, keeping to the right of the wooded 'bump' jutting out into the field. Cross, carefully, the bridge over the brook.

Once over the other side of the stream, bear left and walk parallel to it, towards the gap in the hedge. This is a very peaceful area and worth enjoying for a few minutes. Once through the gap, turn half-right to pass through a stile. Then walk to the top right-hand corner of the field. Turn left, once you have got through the hedge, and walk up to the paddock. Pass through the stiles to enter and then leave the paddock. Walk down the hedged path to come out into the village of Lees itself. On the opposite side of the green is the Black Cow.

28 Dale
The Carpenter's Arms

The Carpenter's Arms stands rather proudly on its own at the northern side of the village of Dale, an attractive small village about 5 miles from the centre of Derby. The pub has been in the same family for the past 60 years and has a friendly village atmosphere.

The food is simple and wholesome and the landlord has developed a menu that is very popular with his customers. It includes plaice, chicken, scampi, home-made steak and ale pie, chilli con carne and curry. The pub has many regular visitors, so the proof must be in the pudding. The real ales (draught Burton Ale plus a guest ale) are good too. Strongbow draught cider is available and in good weather you can make use of the beer garden. There is also a family room.

Telephone: 0602 325277.

How to get there: Dale lies just off the A6096, between Ilkeston and Spondon (on the A52, 2 miles east of Derby). The pub is on your left as you enter the village.

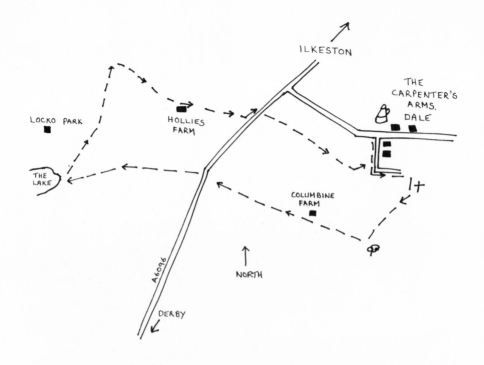

Parking: The landlord has no objection to you using the pub car park, while you walk, as long as you ask him first. There is also some parking on the road running away from the front of the pub.

Length of the walk: 4¾ miles. Map: OS Pathfinder 833 Nottingham (South West) (GR 436389).

Anyone used to walking in the Peak District would do well to explore this area to the north-east of Derby as well. The countryside is interesting and attractive and the paths are good. There are no difficult climbs on the walk and it is a pleasant, easy route.

The Walk

From the Carpenter's Arms, walk straight down the lane in front of the pub. This leads to a grass triangle at the bottom. Bear left at this point, walking round the corner past the Abbey House. To your left you should be able to see the remains of Dale Abbey built, supposedly, on the site where a medieval outlaw saw a vision of a golden cross. Follow the lane round until you come to the church. An unusual black and white timber building, All Saints forms part of a structure which

118

is also a private house. Stay to the right of the church and the house. At the side of the conservatory, bear right (at the bridleway signpost for Dunnshill a mile away). Do not go into the farmyard. In the first field, walk uphill to the gate on the left, which is waymarked. In the next field, follow the holly hedge as it bears round to the right.

Enter Ockbrook Wood and walk along the bottom side of it towards Columbine Farm. Ignore the path to the left, uphill in the wood. At the end of the wood, pass through the gate. Follow the bridleway past the sign saying 'No picnics' (erected by the Locko Park Estate Office). Ahead is Columbine Farm. Do not head for the farm but keep to the left of it. Walk towards the gate at the bottom of a small wooded hill. Climb the stile at the side of the gate and follow the track gently downhill, past a barn on the right. Turn left along the farm drive. Follow the drive for approximately ½ mile towards the A6096. Go through a gateway just before the road. Where the tarmac track bears right, keep straight on up a sunken lane.

Cross the A6096 and walk up the track on the right of the house in front. Follow the public bridleway sign to Locko Park. Keep on this bridleway for 750 yards to bring you to Lodge Farm on the left. Stay on the tarmac track until you come to the lake.

The route of the walk bears back to the right at an acute angle but you may wish to take a break at this point and look at the wildfowl on the water. The bridleway continues along the left-hand side of the lake, so feel free to carry on a little further before returning to the eastern end of the lake.

The walk now follows the footpath heading off to the right from the line you walked down from the road. So, at the side of the driveway heading up to the impressive house of Locko Park, go through the kissing-gate and proceed towards the wood on the hillside. The path should be visible. Climb over the stile into the wood. Pass through the wood and out the other side. You can see Locko Park itself to the left. Pass through the kissing-gate at the edge of the wood. Walk towards a second wood in front, keeping the fence on your right. Cross the wooden footbridge and head forward to the right-hand corner of the field. Pass through the line of trees, keeping straight ahead to the right of the third wood. In the corner, climb over into the field on your right – this stile is not easy to see until you reach it. Turn left and walk past the wood on your left. Carry on along the left-hand side of this field and the next until you come to a track.

At this track, turn left through a gateway and immediately turn right. Follow the waymark through the gate and keep on the right-hand side of the field. Away to the left can be seen a windmill – one of only a handful in the area (and most of them are in disrepair). At the end of the field, pass through the bridlegate. Keep on beside the hedge on your right, passing through the gateway into the next field towards a green lane. Follow this for the next 450 yards or so, then follow the blue waymarks towards Hollies Farm. With the hedge on your right, walk up the track towards the farm, then bear left in front of it, with the fencing on your right. Pass through the gate and follow the blue waymarks through the farmyard, with the barn on your left.

Take the track leading away from the farm towards Flourish Farm ahead. The bridleway brings you back out onto the A6096, to the right of the farm. Turn left along the road, walking in the direction of the windmill in the distance for just under 200 yards. Just past the house known as 'One The Flourish', look out for the farmgate on the opposite side of the road. Cross the road to this gate (there is a signpost hidden in the hedge) and enter the field. Walk along the track down the middle of the field, towards the gate. Stay on this track through the next two fields. At the end of the second field, cross through the stile (avoiding the muck heap) and carry on through the centre of the field towards the far corner, with the church at Dale beyond.

Climb over the stile and walk along the well-used path, ignoring the stile on your right through the hedge. The path leads you to a wooden fence. Turn right at the end of this and climb a step-over stile. Stay on the path, with a fence on your right and a hedge on the left. Pass through a little gate and turn left, then walk through the brick arch into the garden of The Byre. Take the gate on the left and walk down the pebble track to the road, past the old stone building on your right. This used to be a lock-up in which prisoners were kept whilst being moved from one place to another. Once back on the road, turn left towards the Carpenter's Arms at the end.

㉙ Ingleby
The John Thompson

For the origin of the name of the John Thompson inn you need look no further than its present landlord, John Thompson. Not many landlords can claim the distinction of having their pub named after them. Originally this 500-year-old building was a farmhouse, the oak beams attesting to this. The land around the inn was farmed by Mr Thompson's parents before he, too, became a farmer and fruit merchant. Then, in 1969, he converted the farmhouse into an inn and started to brew his own beer, actually on the premises, in 1977. There is JTS XXX, as well as either JTS Summergold (in summer) or Porter (in winter). Draught Bass is also available for those who do not want to try a new brew.

The John Thompson is a lovely inn, with lots of unusual features. Both the building itself and the garden are attractive and, in addition, it must surely have the largest collection of Gresley watercolours anywhere. These are local scenes and are worth visiting the inn for in their own right.

There is a no-smoking area, a beer garden and a family room. From Monday to Saturday (inclusive) meals are available from noon to 2.30 pm but no food is served in the evening. Then on Sunday

sandwiches only are served from noon to 2.30 pm. The menu concentrates on traditional items, all well presented. Examples are roast beef, Yorkshire pudding and three vegetables, salad, soup, cold meat buffet, jacket potatoes and a selection of sweets and gâteaux.
Telephone: 0332 862469.

How to get there: Ingleby can be reached from the A514, south of Derby. A mile or so after leaving Chellaston, the road bears round sharply to the left to cross the river Trent. Immediately beyond the bridge, turn right. Ignoring all roads off to the left, this road brings you about 1 ½ miles later to the John Thompson inn on the right, with the flag of St George flying proudly in the gardens.

Parking: There is a large car park at the inn and parking there, while you walk, should not be a problem, but check first with the landlord.

Length of the walk: 4 ½ miles. Map: OS Pathfinder 852 Burton-upon-Trent (GR 354269).

The walk takes you through a fascinating part of the county, full of history. In an area dominated by the Danes many centuries ago, Ingleby ('Farm of the Angles') probably denotes an isolated group of Englishmen amongst the Danish majority. This is a fairly flat circuit largely over fields and tracks.

The Walk
From the John Thompson, turn right up the lane towards the village. After just over ⅓ mile, the road bears quite sharply to the left. Just round the corner at the public bridleway sign, pass through the gate. Head towards the gate in the far right-hand corner of the field, keeping the wall and fence on your right. Beyond this second gate the bridleway and path fork – take the footpath to the right. There are now good views of the river Trent. Keep on through the next few fields, with the fence on your left and the river on your right. After a short distance the path is quite high above the river. Willington Power Station looms on the horizon, 2 or 3 miles ahead. The path drops back towards the river. Bear left alongside a long pond and follow this, with the pond on your right and rocks on your left. After a short distance the path leads to Anchor church. This was the home of an ancient hermit who carved his home out of the rock face.
    Walk to the end of the pond and, beyond the rocks, cross over the fence. Carry straight on to the right of some more rocks in front. Walk forward towards Hill Plantation, with the trees 400 yards ahead. When you reach a track just before the plantation, ignoring the stile on your left, climb the stile to the right of a gate. Walk up Windmill Hill, across

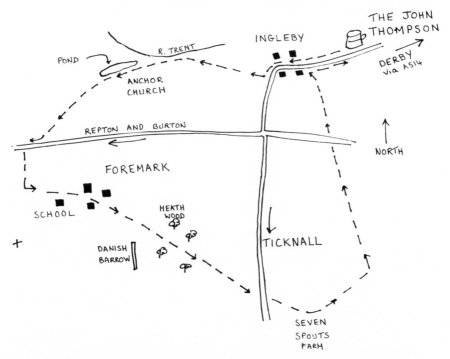

the field in front of you towards the telegraph pole. Keep straight on from this to the stile onto the road. This stile may be slightly difficult to see, but as long as you head in a straight line from the track to the telegraph pole and straight on from there you will find it. If there is a crop on Windmill Hill, you are within your rights to walk the path, even if you cannot see any sign of it on the ground. Some walkers appear to walk on the track along the right-hand side of this field when the path over the hill is difficult to follow.

Once you are on the road, turn right and, 150 yards later, turn left up the track, after passing some trees on the left. This leads to Repton Preparatory School. Walk along the track, taking the first left along another track between trees. Although there is a sign saying 'Foremark Hall: Private Road', this is a public footpath. Shortly this path will take you past playing fields on your left and then past a pond. Now on your right is Foremark Hall. In front of the Hall, follow the tarmac drive all the way through the school outbuildings. At the letterbox and telephone box, take the track to the right, walking alongside the red-brick wall. Keep on this track, between the avenue of trees, for 500 yards. Just before you enter Heath Wood, look right. You will see what appears to be a small conifer plantation. In fact, hidden by the trees is a Danish barrow cemetery. Unfortunately, there is no right of way to the barrow.

Walk through Heath Wood. There are usually many pheasants here. At the end of the wood, keep straight on along the track to the road. Cross the road and head down the track opposite, towards Seven Spouts Farm. Just past the farm there is a choice of three tracks. Take the one to the left, which then bears round to the left. Follow along the well defined path through the trees, passing a pond on your right. About 200 yards beyond the end of the pond, there is a crossroads of tracks. Your walk follows the bridleway to the left through the bridlegate. Walk uphill, slightly to the right of straight ahead, from this bridlegate to the far right-hand corner of the field. Once there follow the track straight ahead to the tarmac lane.

Pass through the double gates opposite (by the bridleway signpost) and keep down the left-hand side of the hedge in front. At the end of this field (just before the double gate), turn right through the smaller gate into a copse, then follow the track into the grounds of an attractive house. Keeping the house on your left, walk down the drive to the road.

You are now back in the village and can turn right and head back to the John Thompson.

③⓪ Ticknall
The Staff of Life

This interesting inn is a 15th century red-brick building that used to be a bakery. At one stage, in addition to being a bakery, it was also a pig farm and a pub! It was even called the Loaf of Bread at one time. There is a benevolent ghost, understood to be a former landlady, who still tidies up after everyone else has gone to bed. This particular landlady, a Mrs Soar, was obviously a character. She had a key to the village lock-up and she used to let the drunks out after they had been locked in.

The Staff of Life's menu includes steak and kidney pie, moussaka, biryani turkey steak (hot!), chicken tikka, tuna and pasta bake and cheeseburger in a bap – just six of the 28 meals available daily. Then there are another 13 available at all sessions except Sunday lunch (quiche lorraine, gammon and egg or pineapple, breaded scampi and sausages and egg, for example). About another 15 meals are available evenings only, such as lamb with orange and ginger, venison in red wine sauce, chicken breast with prawns and lobster. In addition, there are children's meals, snacks, starters and desserts, and a three-course traditional Sunday lunch. The gammon is a speciality – mention of a 30 oz gammon steak has been made. From Monday to Saturday (inclusive) meals are served from 11.30 am to 1.45 pm and from 6.45 pm to 9.45 pm. On Sunday, noon to 1.45 pm and 7 pm to 9.45 pm. The Staff of Life is a real ale drinker's paradise. Timothy Taylor Landlord, Bishops Finger, Theakston XB and Old Peculier and Marston's Pedigree are usually available, plus guest beers. Strongbow and Woodpecker draught ciders are also served. There is a family room, a beer garden and a garden area with swings.

Telephone: 0332 862479.

How to get there: Ticknall is on the A514, south of Derby. In the village itself, take the B5006 for Smisby and Ashby. The Staff of Life is only 50 or 60 yards beyond the turn.

Parking: The pub car park is small but you can park there, while you walk, provided you use the pub. Please ask first though. There is also street parking along the road near the pub.

Length of the walk: 4½ miles. Map: OS Pathfinder 852 Burton-upon-Trent (GR 351238).

The combination of pub and walk is ideal. The food is excellent and the scenery attractive. This is a flat route with no hills. It is a lovely walk in all seasons, especially in the autumn or on a crisp winter's day. Halfway round you will pass close to Calke Abbey.

The Walk

From the Staff of Life, with the church away to your right, turn left uphill along the road. Look out for the footpath approximately 100 yards past the pub. Turn left at the footpath sign and walk along the gennell (or ginnel or jitty, whichever you prefer). Keep straight ahead, with the wall and hedge on your right. At the corner of the wall, bear slightly right towards the far corner of the field. Cross the stile in the corner of this field and then walk across to the stile on the opposite side of the field. From here, walk nearly parallel to the fence on your

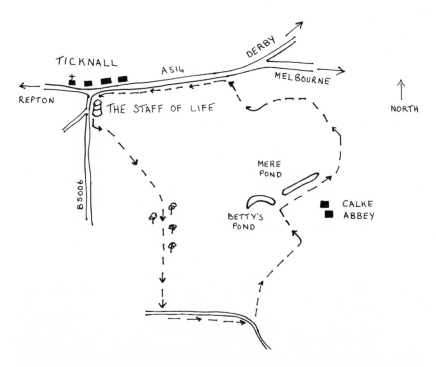

left towards the big tree opposite. A hedge has been removed hereabouts and so it may be slightly difficult to relate the lie of the land to the OS map. It appears that two fields have been made into one.

Climb over the stile beside the large tree and into the parkland. Bear slightly left toward the telegraph pole 100 yards away, but, before you reach it, look out for the wide, shallow depression in the ground. Keep to the left of this as well as to the left of the pit. Ahead you will see an archway. Bear away to the right of this towards the second of two gates to the right. Pass through the stile at the side of this and walk along the top side of the field, with the hedge on your left. This hedge soon becomes woodland. At the end of the field, the path follows a track through the trees for 100 yards. Keep along the track on the left-hand side of the next two fields. At the end of the second field, climb over the stile. You should keep almost straight ahead towards the gap between the middle and right hand of three trees across the other side of the field. As you get nearer to these trees you will see a signpost. Climb over the stile on to the lane.

Turn left along the tarmac lane and walk past Standley's Barn. Look out for deer on this farm. Ignore the path to Smisby on the right. Where the lane turns sharply right, turn left along the track. Ignore the path to Heath End. Keep on the track for just over ½ mile. The footpath along this track shown on many OS maps has been diverted and does not continue directly to Calke Abbey along the track you are on. After passing through a small gate at the side of a larger white gate, a tarmac drive joins the track you are on from the left. You should keep straight ahead towards Calke Abbey which ought to be visible in front of you.

Approximately 150 yards along the tarmac drive, on your left, is a mound surmounted by fir trees. Although this looks as though it may be an ancient tumulus (or burial mound), a yellow sign on the fence around it states 'Fire Brigade Culvert Pumping Point 35'. Just about 150 yards beyond this (and still on the tarmac drive), you will see an oak tree at either side of the drive. Once you are between them, turn left off the drive and walk to the right of the oak tree on your left. Walk along a line between a water trough and a seat.

After passing between the trough and the seat, head towards a netting fence which runs on a line away from you. Walking along the left-hand side of the fence, you should see signs of a path on the ground which runs downhill towards the ponds in the valley bottom. Just before the pond to your left, climb over the stile (or pass through the small gate at the side of the stile). Once over the stile, turn right immediately and climb over another stile at the side of the 6 ft high metal gate. Walk along the gravel path before climbing some wooden steps. The path continues along the bank above Mere Pond, below to your left. This is a lovely stretch of the walk and it is worthwhile taking your time to admire the beautiful countryside.

Where the gravel path forks, take the left-hand path down towards the pond and pass through a kissing-gate. Follow the path alongside the pond until you come to a deer fence. Turn left over a bridge and proceed alongside the fence, climbing slowly uphill. At the track at the end of the wood, turn left and then, 30 yards later, pass through a gap in the wall on your right. Walk across the field towards the cottage (White Leys) in the far left corner of the field. Cross the private driveway and follow the footpath to the right of the cottage. The path bears round to the left. At the end of the field, pass through the gateway so that you are now walking towards the wood with the hedge on your right. The path becomes a track. Follow this into the wood, and continue until you reach the road. Turn left along this into the village, passing under Horseshoe Bridge and by an old lock-up, before turning left back to the Staff of Life.

If you wish to visit Calke Abbey after your walk, it is open from the beginning of April to the end of October, Saturday to Wednesday (including Bank Holiday Monday) from 1 pm to 5.30 pm. Times may vary so contact the Abbey on 0332 864444/863822 to check.